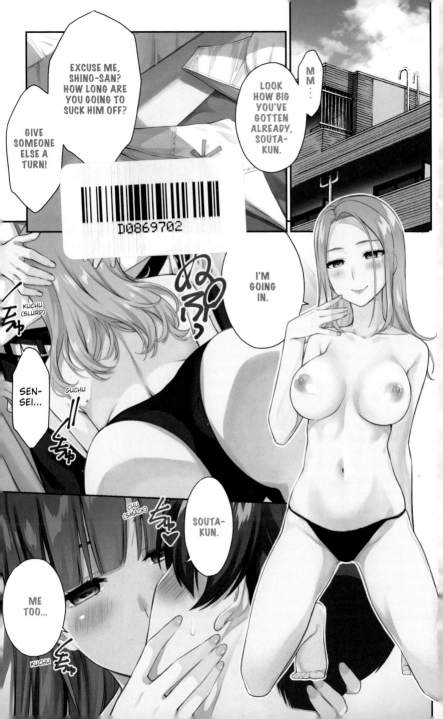

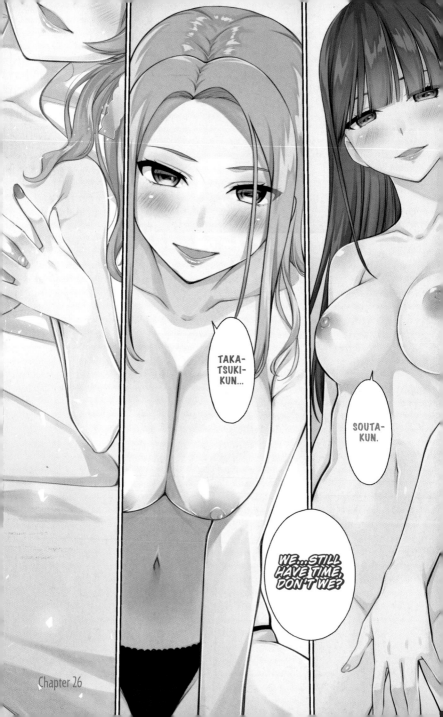

Chapter 26

Lust Geass

[5]

contents

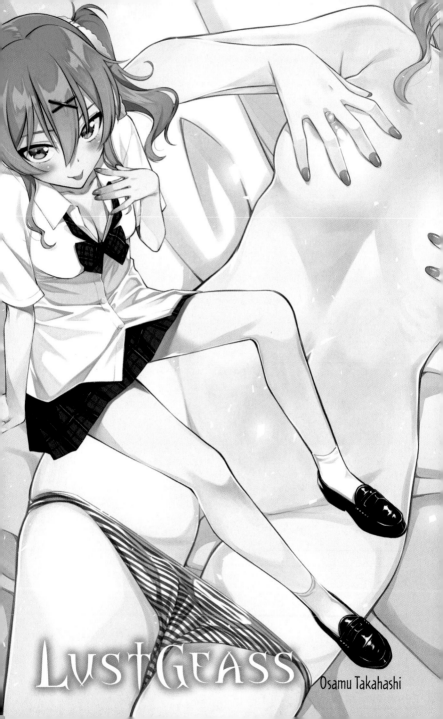

LustGeass

Osamu Takahashi

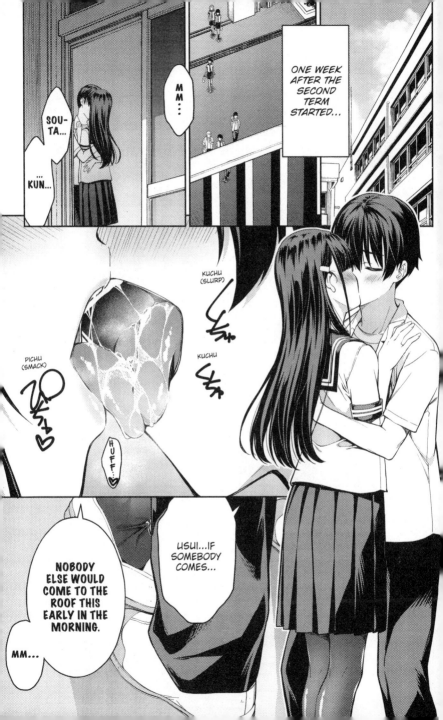

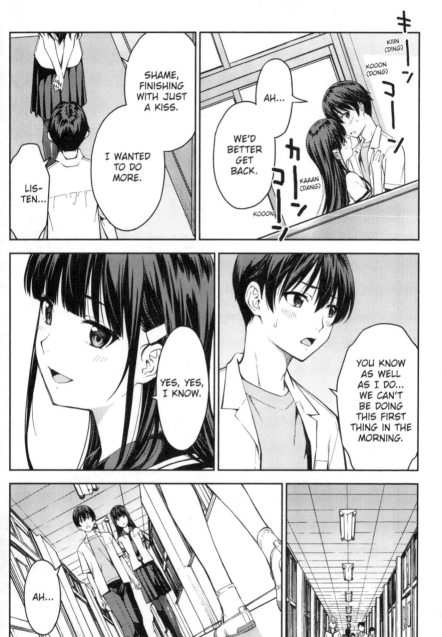

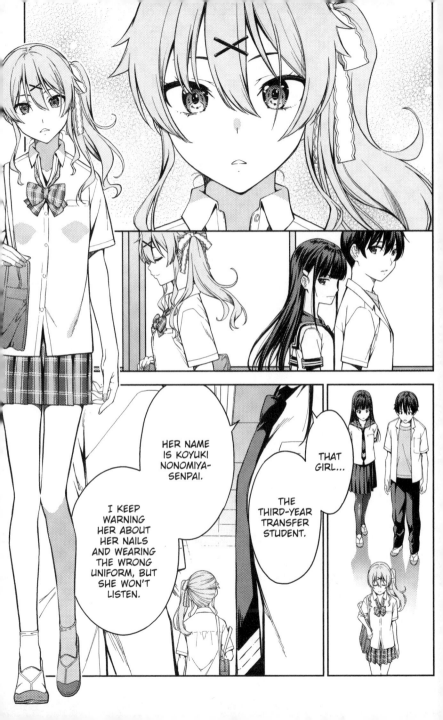

HER NAME IS KOYUKI NONOMIYA-SENPAI.

I KEEP WARNING HER ABOUT HER NAILS AND WEARING THE WRONG UNIFORM, BUT SHE WON'T LISTEN.

THAT GIRL...

THE THIRD-YEAR TRANSFER STUDENT.

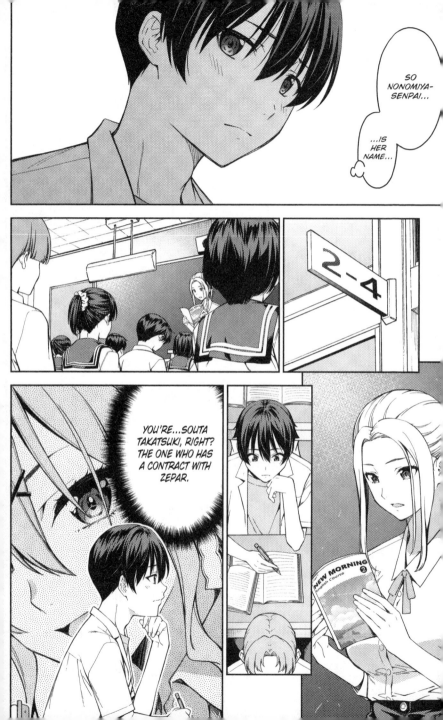

SO NONOMIYA-SENPAI...

...IS HER NAME...

2-4

YOU'RE...SOUTA TAKATSUKI, RIGHT? THE ONE WHO HAS A CONTRACT WITH ZEPAR.

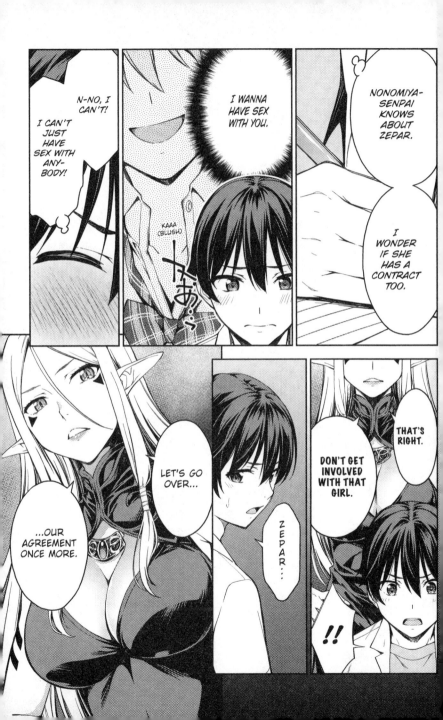

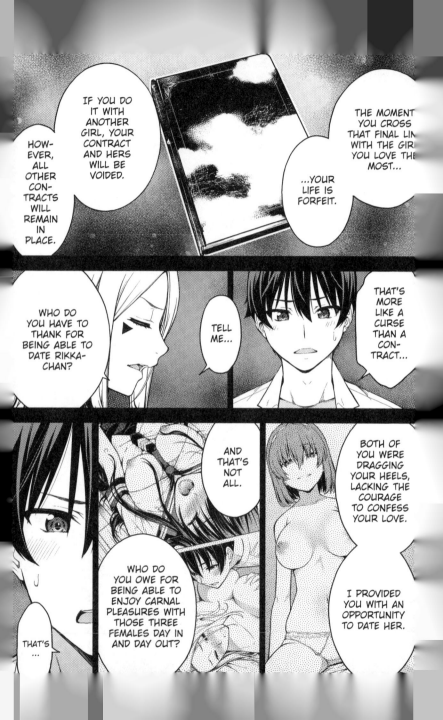

IF YOU DO IT WITH ANOTHER GIRL, YOUR CONTRACT AND HERS WILL BE VOIDED.

HOW-EVER, ALL OTHER CON-TRACTS WILL REMAIN IN PLACE.

THE MOMENT YOU CROSS THAT FINAL LINE WITH THE GIRL YOU LOVE THE MOST...

...YOUR LIFE IS FORFEIT.

WHO DO YOU HAVE TO THANK FOR BEING ABLE TO DATE RIKKA-CHAN?

TELL ME...

THAT'S MORE LIKE A CURSE THAN A CON-TRACT...

AND THAT'S NOT ALL.

BOTH OF YOU WERE DRAGGING YOUR HEELS, LACKING THE COURAGE TO CONFESS YOUR LOVE.

WHO DO YOU OWE FOR BEING ABLE TO ENJOY CARNAL PLEASURES WITH THOSE THREE FEMALES DAY IN AND DAY OUT?

I PROVIDED YOU WITH AN OPPORTUNITY TO DATE HER.

THAT'S ...

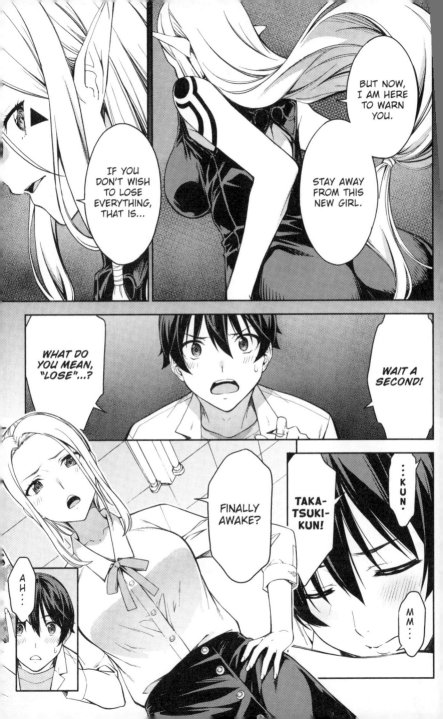

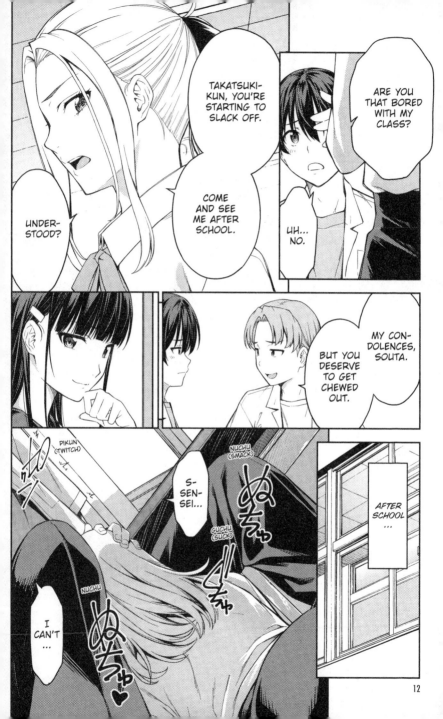

TAKATSUKI-KUN, YOU'RE STARTING TO SLACK OFF.

ARE YOU THAT BORED WITH MY CLASS?

UNDER-STOOD?

COME AND SEE ME AFTER SCHOOL.

UH... NO.

MY CON-DOLENCES, SOUTA.

BUT YOU DESERVE TO GET CHEWED OUT.

PIKUN (TWITCH)

NUCHU (SMACK)

S-SEN-SEI...

GUCHU (SUCK)

NUCHU

I CAN'T...

AFTER SCHOOL...

12

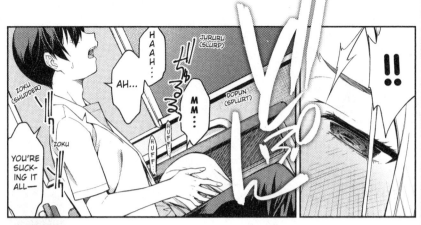

HAAH...

AH...

MM...

JURURU (SLURP)

DOPUN (SPLURT)

ZOKU (SHUDDER)

ZOKU

!!

YOU'RE SUCKING IT ALL—

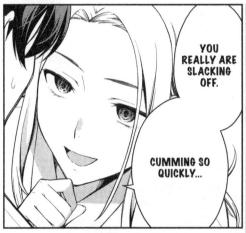

YOU REALLY ARE SLACKING OFF.

CUMMING SO QUICKLY...

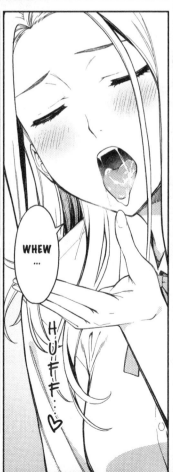

WHEW...

HUFF

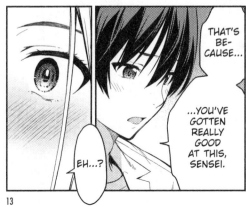

THAT'S BE- CAUSE...

...YOU'VE GOTTEN REALLY GOOD AT THIS, SENSEI.

EH...?

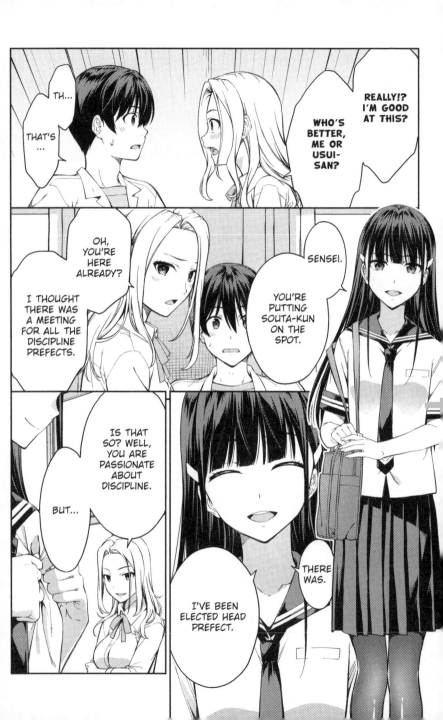

TH...

THAT'S...

WHO'S BETTER, ME OR USUI-SAN?

REALLY!? I'M GOOD AT THIS?

OH, YOU'RE HERE ALREADY?

I THOUGHT THERE WAS A MEETING FOR ALL THE DISCIPLINE PREFECTS.

SENSEI.

YOU'RE PUTTING SOUTA-KUN ON THE SPOT.

IS THAT SO? WELL, YOU ARE PASSIONATE ABOUT DISCIPLINE.

BUT...

THERE WAS.

I'VE BEEN ELECTED HEAD PREFECT.

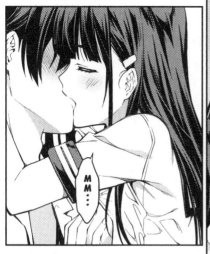

MM...

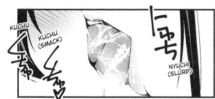

KUCHU

KUCHU
(SMACK)

NYUCHU
(SLURP)

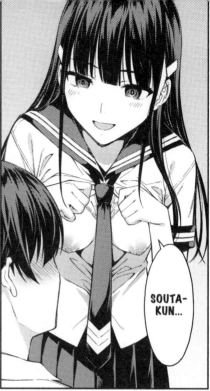

SOUTA-KUN...

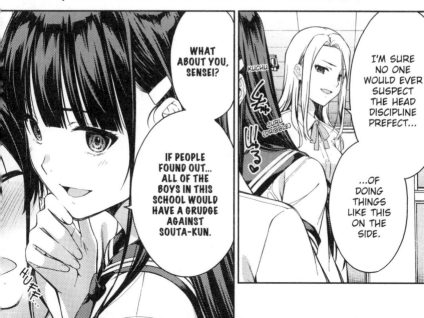

WHAT ABOUT YOU, SENSEI?

IF PEOPLE FOUND OUT... ALL OF THE BOYS IN THIS SCHOOL WOULD HAVE A GRUDGE AGAINST SOUTA-KUN.

HU杏...

KUCHU

JURU
(DRIBBLE)

I'M SURE NO ONE WOULD EVER SUSPECT THE HEAD DISCIPLINE PREFECT...

...OF DOING THINGS LIKE THIS ON THE SIDE.

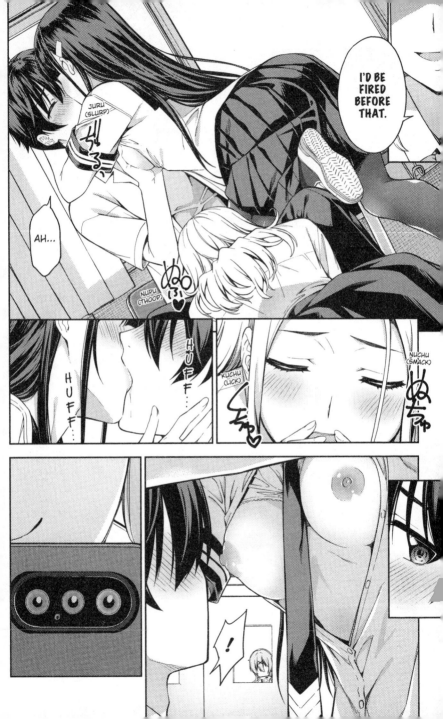

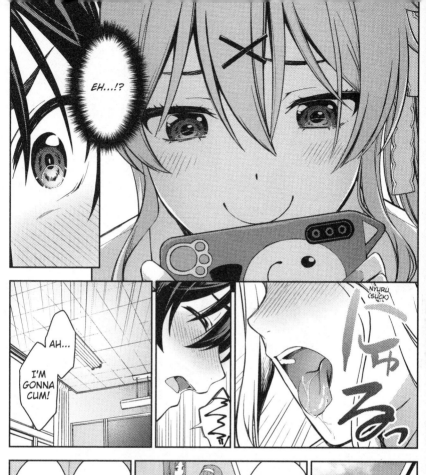

EH...!?

AH...

I'M GONNA CUM!

NYURU (SUCK)

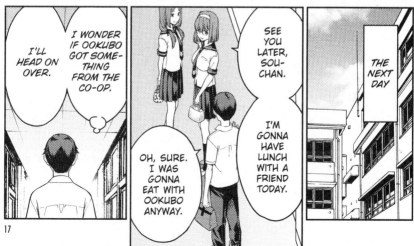

I'LL HEAD ON OVER.

I WONDER IF OOKUBO GOT SOMETHING FROM THE CO-OP.

SEE YOU LATER, SOU-CHAN.

I'M GONNA HAVE LUNCH WITH A FRIEND TODAY.

OH, SURE. I WAS GONNA EAT WITH OOKUBO ANYWAY.

THE NEXT DAY

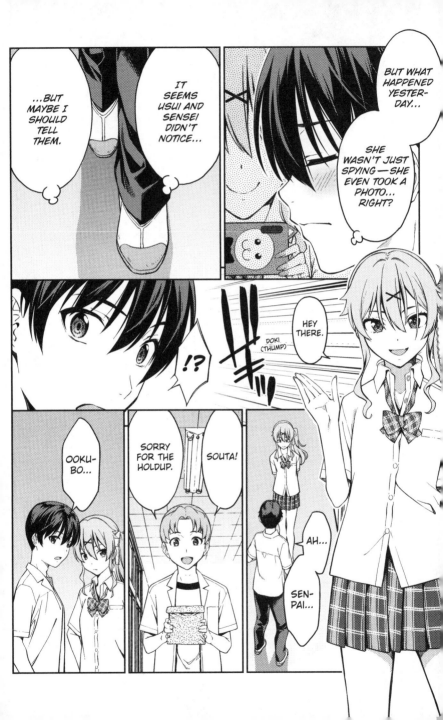

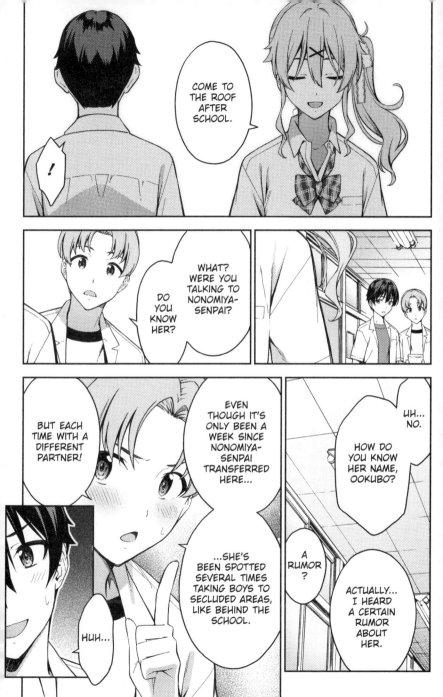

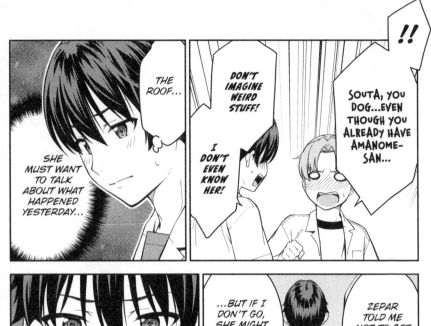

THE ROOF...

SHE MUST WANT TO TALK ABOUT WHAT HAPPENED YESTERDAY...

DON'T IMAGINE WEIRD STUFF!

I DON'T EVEN KNOW HER!

SOUTA, YOU DOG...EVEN THOUGH YOU ALREADY HAVE AMANOME-SAN...

!!

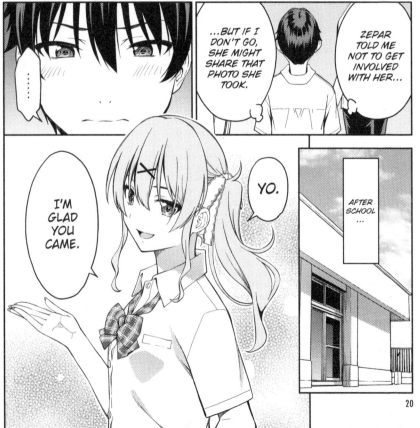

...BUT IF I DON'T GO, SHE MIGHT SHARE THAT PHOTO SHE TOOK.

ZEPAR TOLD ME NOT TO GET INVOLVED WITH HER...

I'M GLAD YOU CAME.

YO.

AFTER SCHOOL...

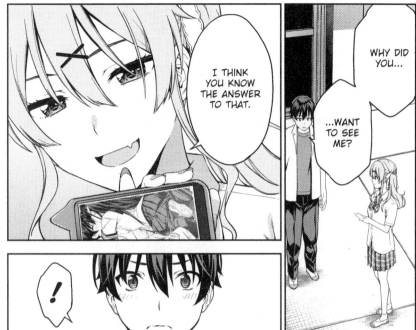

I THINK YOU KNOW THE ANSWER TO THAT.

WHY DID YOU...

...WANT TO SEE ME?

!

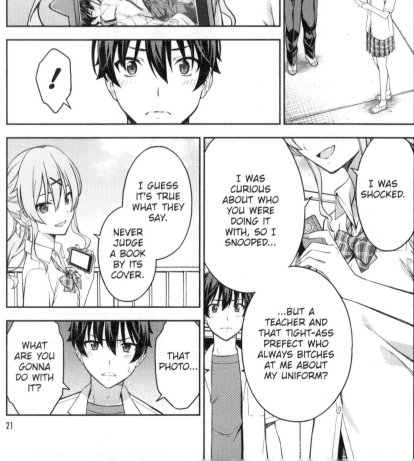

I GUESS IT'S TRUE WHAT THEY SAY.

NEVER JUDGE A BOOK BY ITS COVER.

I WAS CURIOUS ABOUT WHO YOU WERE DOING IT WITH, SO I SNOOPED...

I WAS SHOCKED.

...BUT A TEACHER AND THAT TIGHT-ASS PREFECT WHO ALWAYS BITCHES AT ME ABOUT MY UNIFORM?

WHAT ARE YOU GONNA DO WITH IT?

THAT PHOTO...

HEY... YOU ALREADY KNOW...

...WHAT I WANT, DON'T YOU?

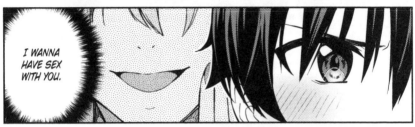

I WANNA HAVE SEX WITH YOU.

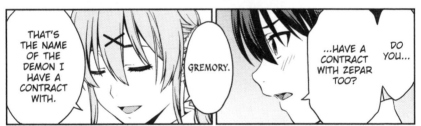

THAT'S THE NAME OF THE DEMON I HAVE A CONTRACT WITH.

GREMORY.

...HAVE A CONTRACT WITH ZEPAR TOO?

DO YOU...

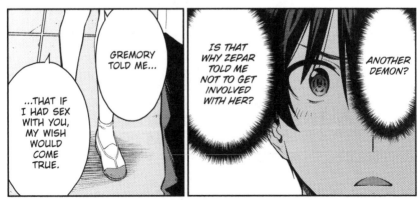

GREMORY TOLD ME...

...THAT IF I HAD SEX WITH YOU, MY WISH WOULD COME TRUE.

IS THAT WHY ZEPAR TOLD ME NOT TO GET INVOLVED WITH HER?

ANOTHER DEMON?

22

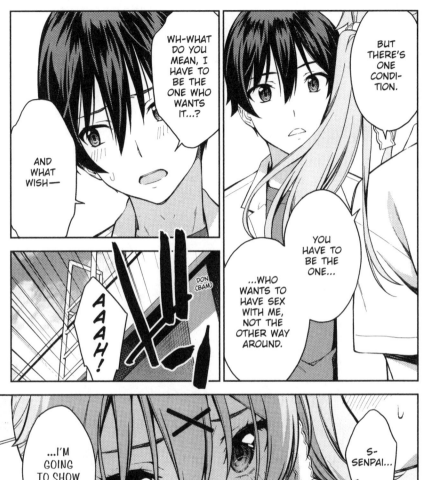

WH-WHAT DO YOU MEAN, I HAVE TO BE THE ONE WHO WANTS IT...?

AND WHAT WISH—

BUT THERE'S ONE CONDITION.

YOU HAVE TO BE THE ONE...

...WHO WANTS TO HAVE SEX WITH ME, NOT THE OTHER WAY AROUND.

AAAH!

DON (BAM)

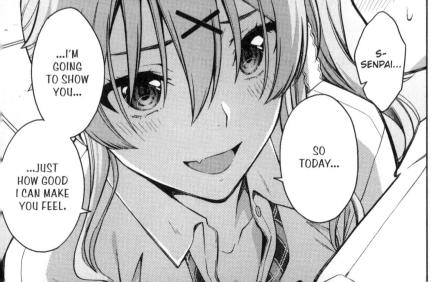

...I'M GOING TO SHOW YOU...

...JUST HOW GOOD I CAN MAKE YOU FEEL.

S-SENPAI...

SO TODAY...

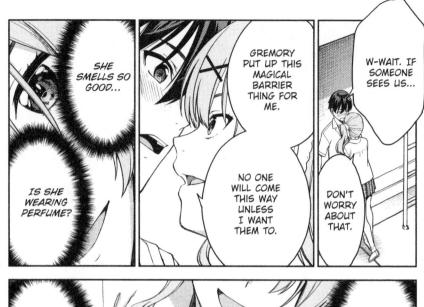

SHE SMELLS SO GOOD...

IS SHE WEARING PERFUME?

GREMORY PUT UP THIS MAGICAL BARRIER THING FOR ME.

NO ONE WILL COME THIS WAY UNLESS I WANT THEM TO.

W-WAIT. IF SOMEONE SEES US...

DON'T WORRY ABOUT THAT.

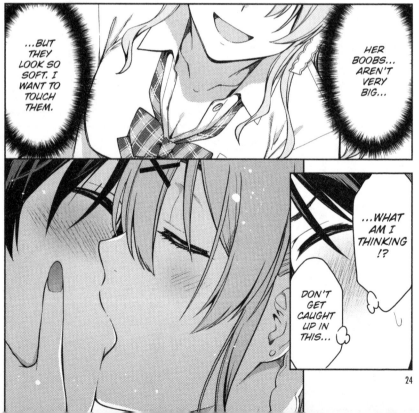

...BUT THEY LOOK SO SOFT. I WANT TO TOUCH THEM.

HER BOOBS... AREN'T VERY BIG...

...WHAT AM I THINKING !?

DON'T GET CAUGHT UP IN THIS...

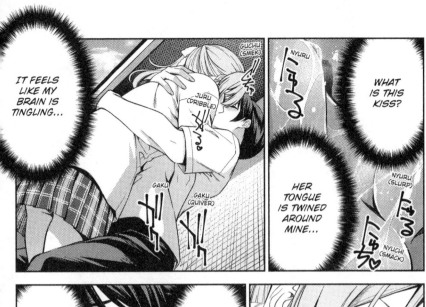

IT FEELS LIKE MY BRAIN IS TINGLING...

GUCHU (SMEK)

JURU (DRIBBLE)

GAKU

GAKU (QUIVER)

WHAT IS THIS KISS?

NYURU

HER TONGUE IS TWINED AROUND MINE...

NYURU (SLURP)

NYUCHI (SMACK)

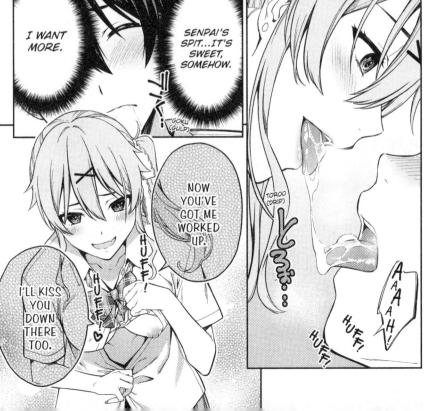

I WANT MORE.

SENPAI'S SPIT...IT'S SWEET, SOMEHOW.

GOKU (GULP)

NOW YOU'VE GOT ME WORKED UP.

I'LL KISS YOU DOWN THERE TOO.

HUFF!

HUFF!

HUFF!

TOROO (DRIP)

AAAAH...

AAAAH!

HUFF!

HUFF!

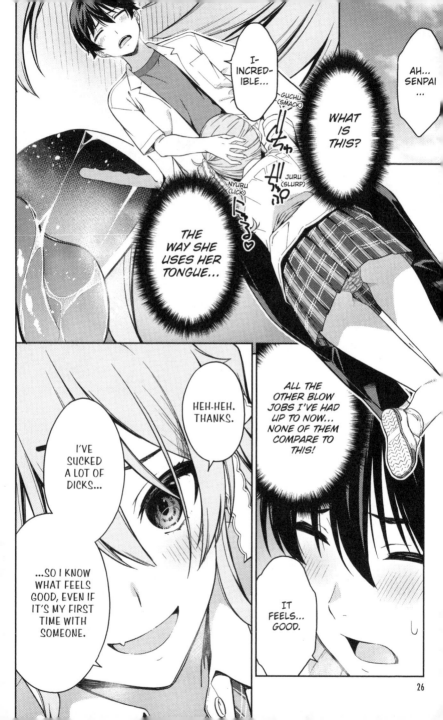

I-INCREDIBLE...

GUCHU (SMACK)

WHAT IS THIS?

AH... SENPAI...

JURU (SLURP)

NYURU (CLICK)

THE WAY SHE USES HER TONGUE...

HEH-HEH. THANKS.

I'VE SUCKED A LOT OF DICKS...

...SO I KNOW WHAT FEELS GOOD, EVEN IF IT'S MY FIRST TIME WITH SOMEONE.

ALL THE OTHER BLOW JOBS I'VE HAD UP TO NOW... NONE OF THEM COMPARE TO THIS!

IT FEELS... GOOD.

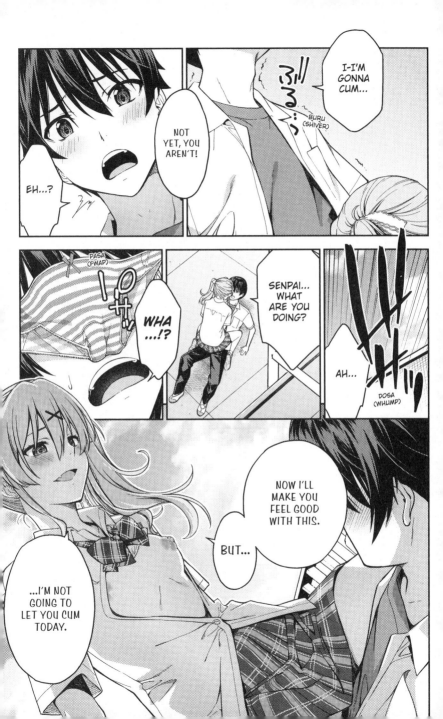

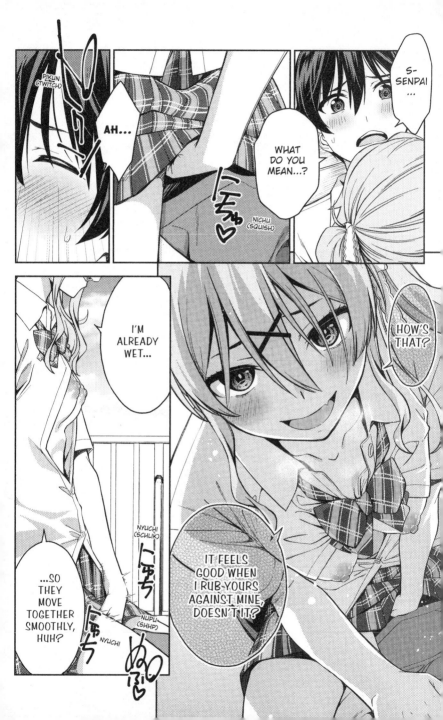

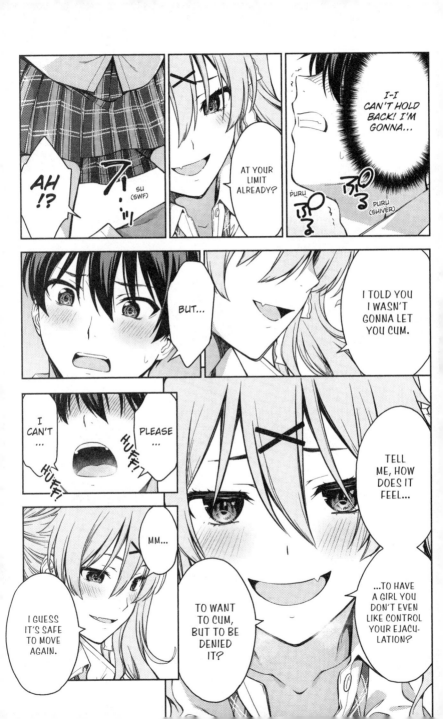

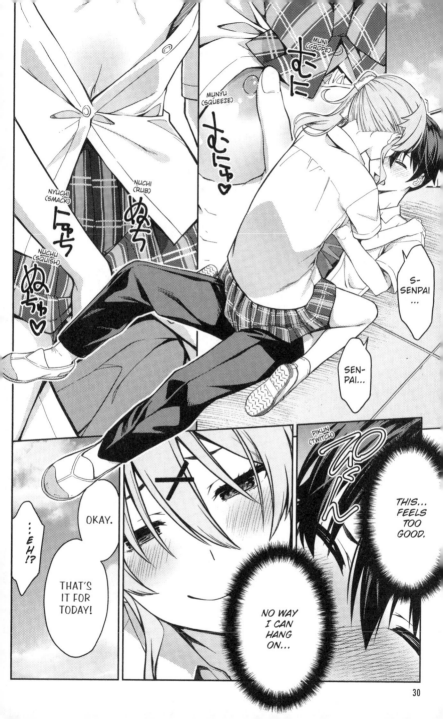

MUNI
(GROPE)

MUNYU
(SQUEEZE)

♥

NYUCHI
(SMACK)

NUCHI
(RUB)

NUCHU
(SQUISH)

♥

S-SENPAI...

SEN-PAI...

PIKUN
(TWITCH)

THIS... FEELS TOO GOOD.

...EH!?

OKAY.

THAT'S IT FOR TODAY!

NO WAY I CAN HANG ON...

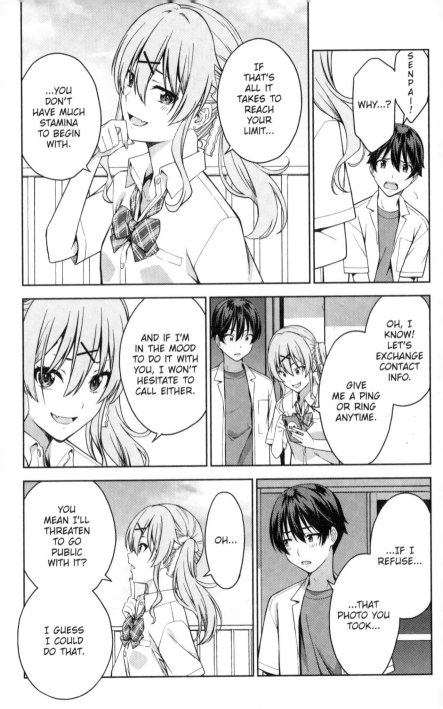

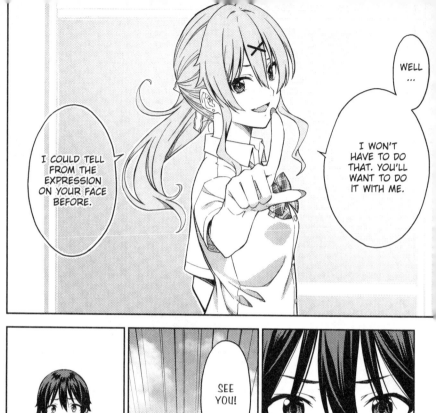

WELL...

I COULD TELL FROM THE EXPRESSION ON YOUR FACE BEFORE.

I WON'T HAVE TO DO THAT. YOU'LL WANT TO DO IT WITH ME.

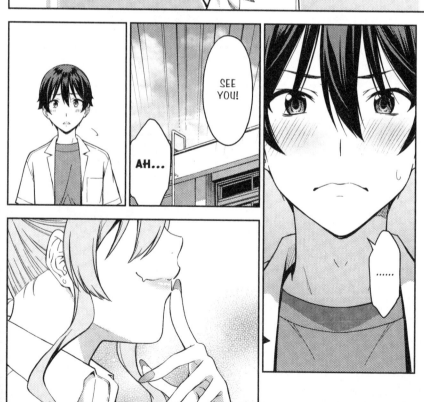

SEE YOU!

AH...

......

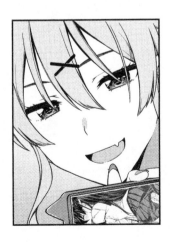

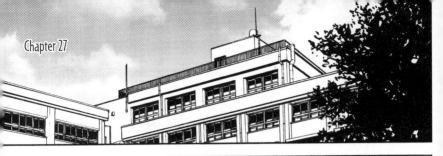

Chapter 27

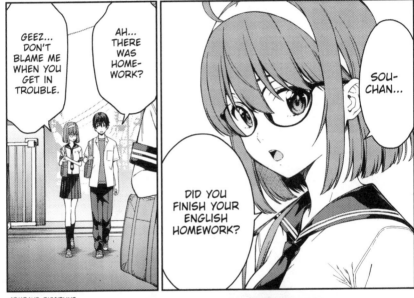

GEEZ... DON'T BLAME ME WHEN YOU GET IN TROUBLE.

AH... THERE WAS HOME-WORK?

SOU-CHAN...

DID YOU FINISH YOUR ENGLISH HOMEWORK?

ARMBAND: DISCIPLINE

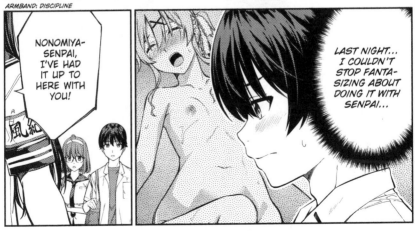

NONOMIYA-SENPAI, I'VE HAD IT UP TO HERE WITH YOU!

LAST NIGHT... I COULDN'T STOP FANTA-SIZING ABOUT DOING IT WITH SENPAI...

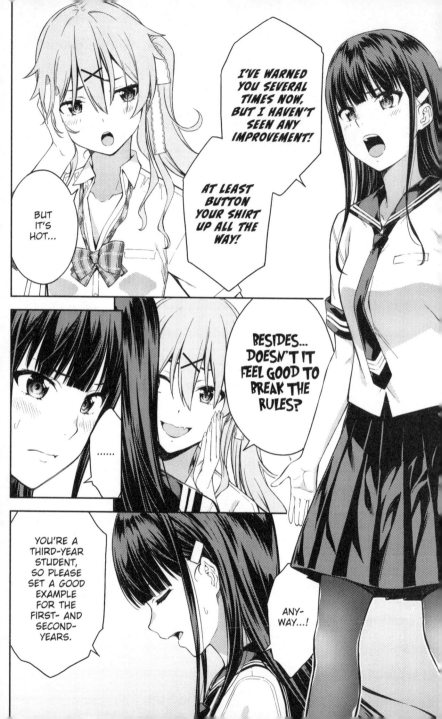

TA
(TMP)

KAAA
(BLUSH)

I'LL TAKE YOUR ADVICE TO HEART.

AH...

SEE YOU LATER, OH-MOST-SERIOUS OF DISCIPLINE PREFECTS!

YOU'VE GOT A HARD JOB, MAKOTO-CHAN.

AH, THAT GIRL... SHE GOT AWAY...

BIII
(BZZZ)

BIII

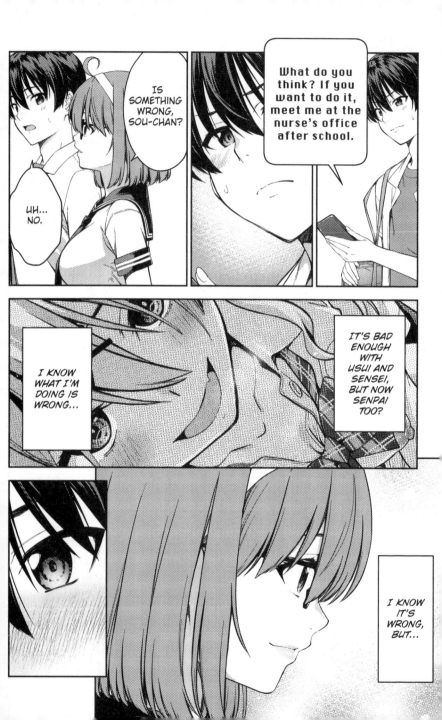

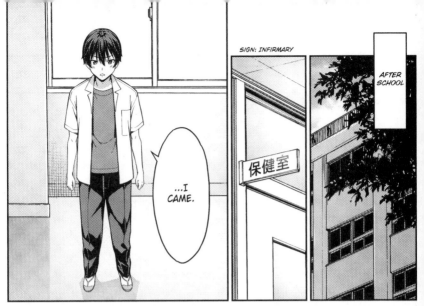

SIGN: INFIRMARY

保健室

AFTER SCHOOL

...I CAME.

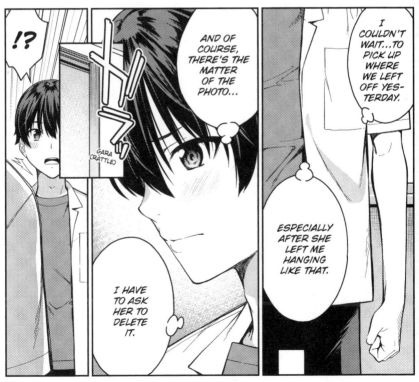

!?

GARA (RATTLE)

AND OF COURSE, THERE'S THE MATTER OF THE PHOTO...

I COULDN'T WAIT...TO PICK UP WHERE WE LEFT OFF YESTERDAY.

ESPECIALLY AFTER SHE LEFT ME HANGING LIKE THAT.

I HAVE TO ASK HER TO DELETE IT.

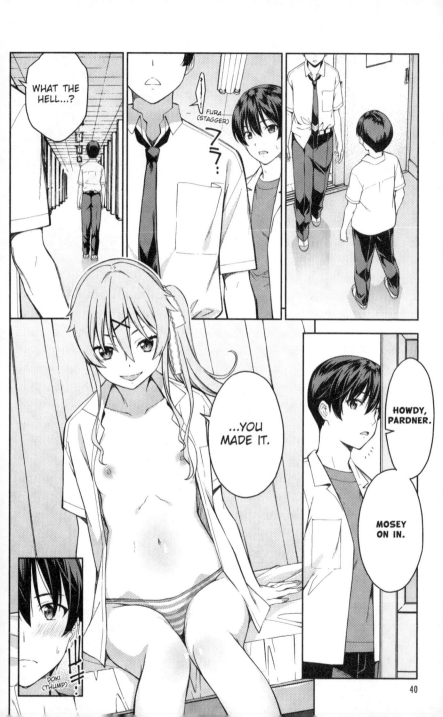

WHAT THE HELL...?

FURA (STAGGER)

...YOU MADE IT.

HOWDY, PARDNER.

MOSEY ON IN.

DOKI (THUMP)

40

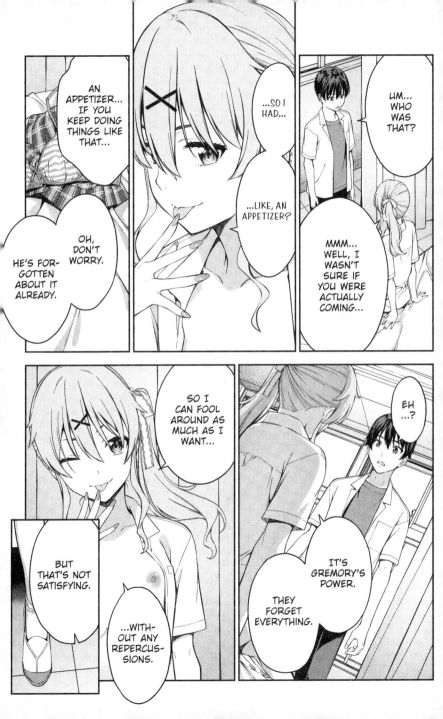

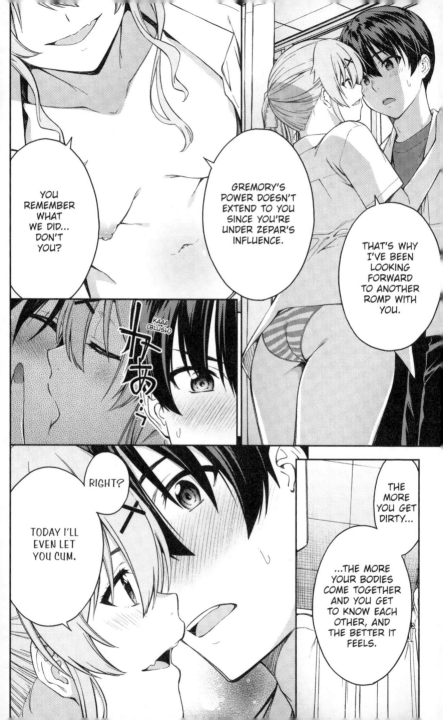

YOU REMEMBER WHAT WE DID... DON'T YOU?

GREMORY'S POWER DOESN'T EXTEND TO YOU SINCE YOU'RE UNDER ZEPAR'S INFLUENCE.

THAT'S WHY I'VE BEEN LOOKING FORWARD TO ANOTHER ROMP WITH YOU.

KAAA (BLUSH)

RIGHT?

TODAY I'LL EVEN LET YOU CUM.

THE MORE YOU GET DIRTY...

...THE MORE YOUR BODIES COME TOGETHER AND YOU GET TO KNOW EACH OTHER, AND THE BETTER IT FEELS.

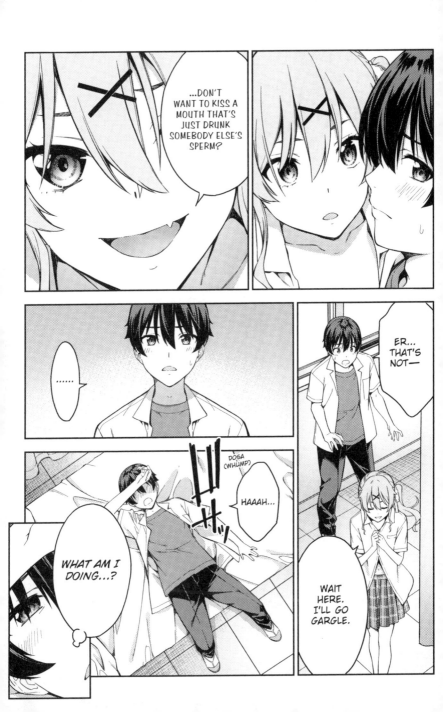

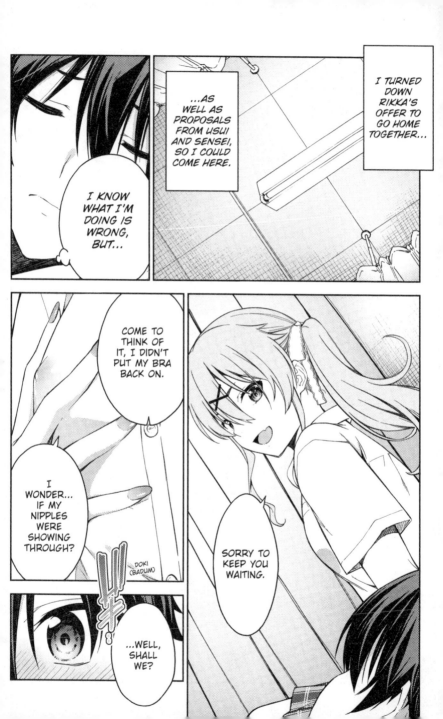

I TURNED DOWN RIKKA'S OFFER TO GO HOME TOGETHER...

...AS WELL AS PROPOSALS FROM USUI AND SENSEI, SO I COULD COME HERE.

I KNOW WHAT I'M DOING IS WRONG, BUT...

COME TO THINK OF IT, I DIDN'T PUT MY BRA BACK ON.

I WONDER... IF MY NIPPLES WERE SHOWING THROUGH?

DOKI
(BADUM)

SORRY TO KEEP YOU WAITING.

...WELL, SHALL WE?

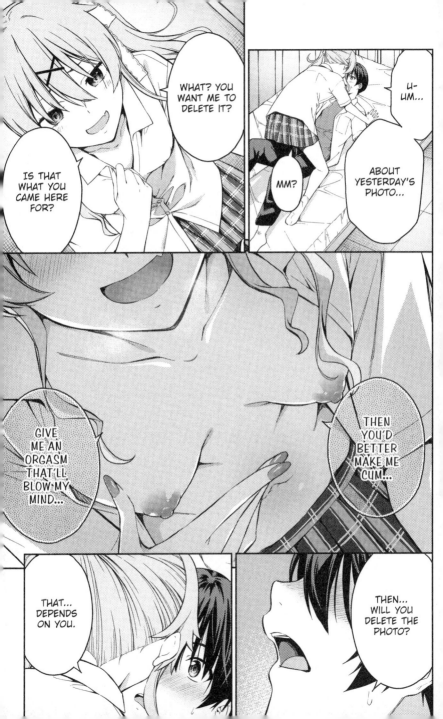

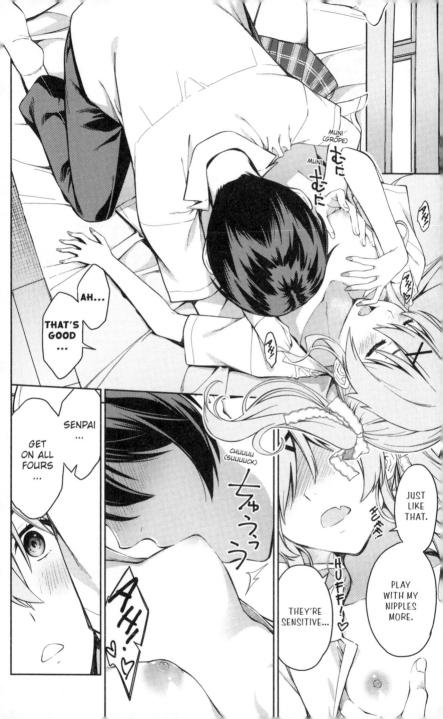

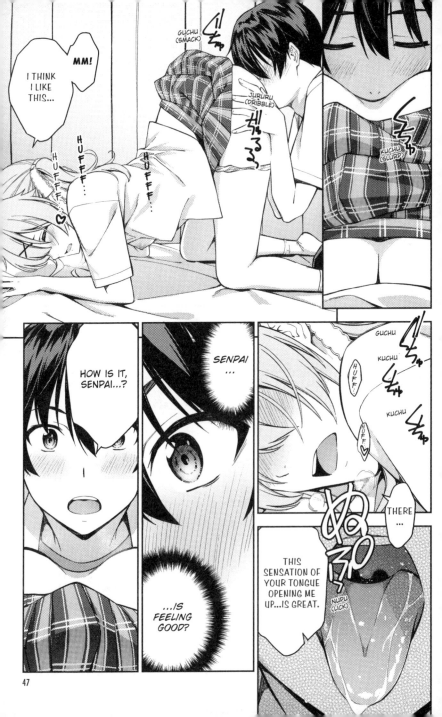

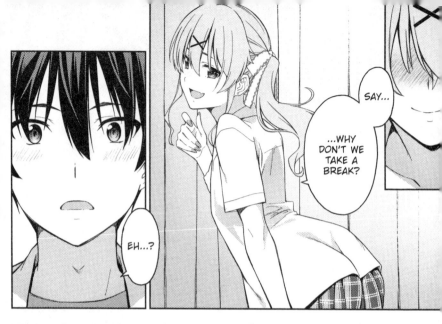

SAY...

...WHY DON'T WE TAKE A BREAK?

EH...?

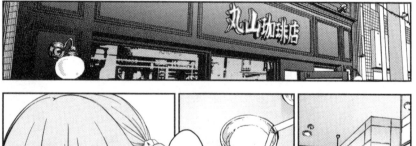

丸山珈琲店

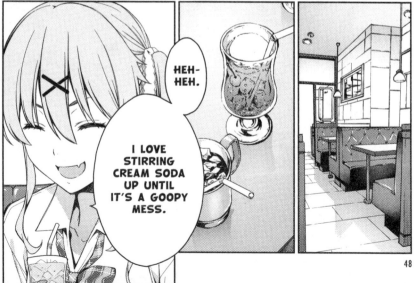

HEH-HEH.

I LOVE STIRRING CREAM SODA UP UNTIL IT'S A GOOPY MESS.

48

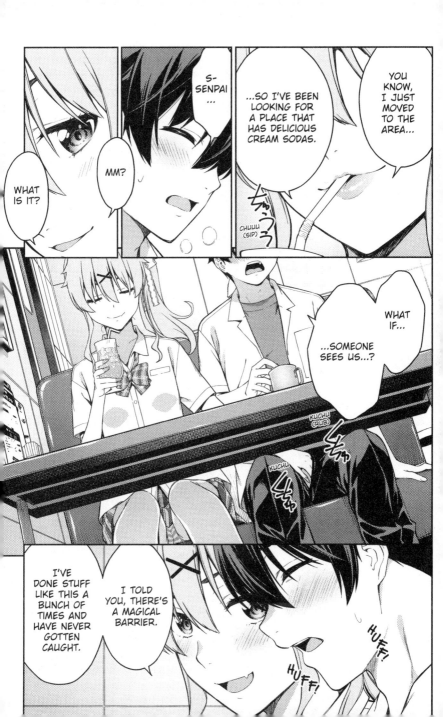

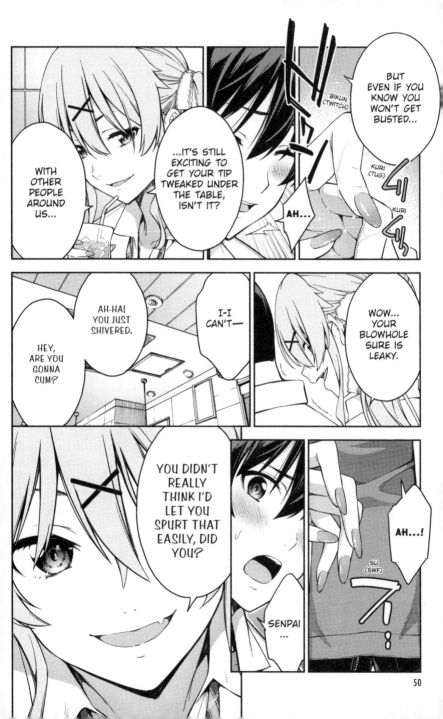

BUT EVEN IF YOU KNOW YOU WON'T GET BUSTED...

BIKUN (TWITCH)

WITH OTHER PEOPLE AROUND US...

...IT'S STILL EXCITING TO GET YOUR TIP TWEAKED UNDER THE TABLE, ISN'T IT?

KURI (TUG)

AH...

KURI

HEY, ARE YOU GONNA CUM?

AH-HA! YOU JUST SHIVERED.

I-I CAN'T—

WOW... YOUR BLOWHOLE SURE IS LEAKY.

YOU DIDN'T REALLY THINK I'D LET YOU SPURT THAT EASILY, DID YOU?

SENPAI...

AH...!

SU (SWF)

50

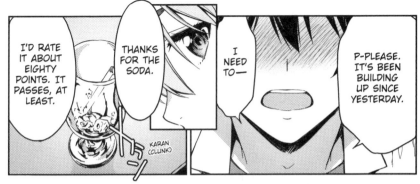

I'D RATE IT ABOUT EIGHTY POINTS. IT PASSES, AT LEAST.

THANKS FOR THE SODA.

KARAN (CLUNK)

I NEED TO—

P-PLEASE. IT'S BEEN BUILDING UP SINCE YESTERDAY.

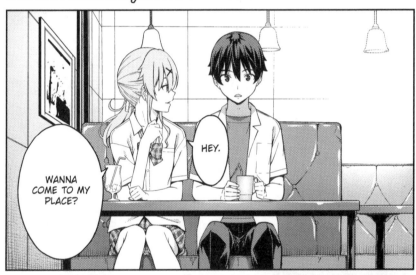

WANNA COME TO MY PLACE?

HEY.

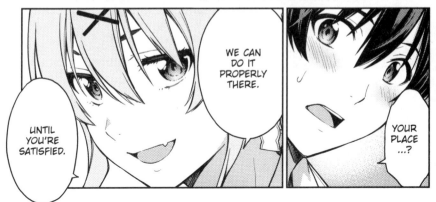

UNTIL YOU'RE SATISFIED.

WE CAN DO IT PROPERLY THERE.

YOUR PLACE ...?

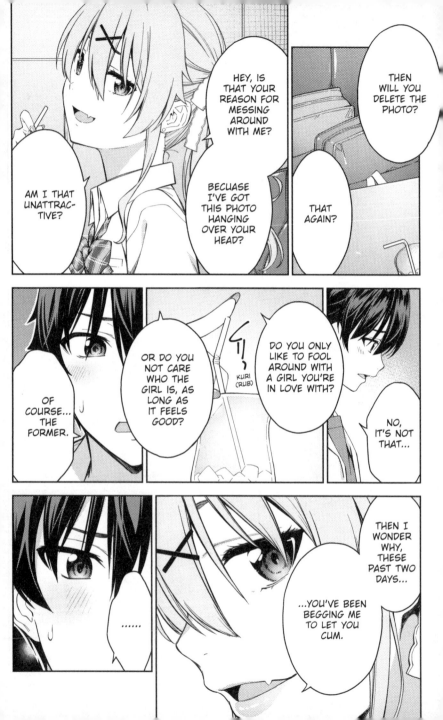

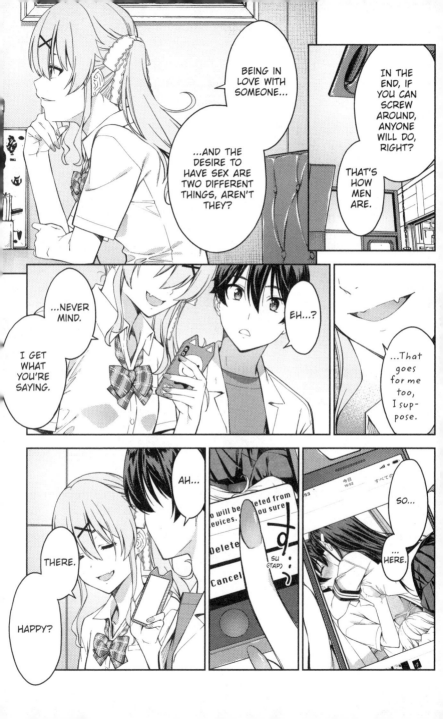

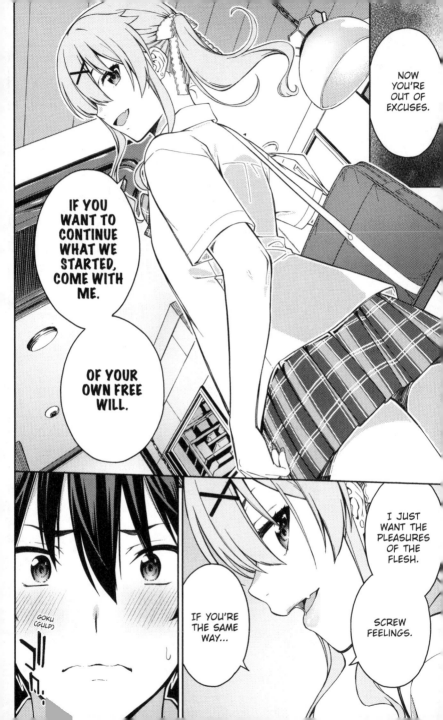

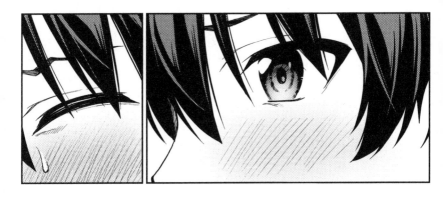

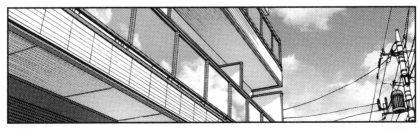

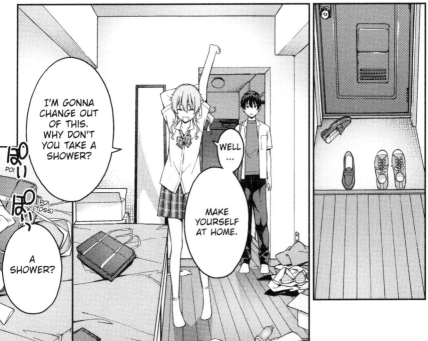

I'M GONNA CHANGE OUT OF THIS. WHY DON'T YOU TAKE A SHOWER?

POI

POI (TOSS)

WELL ...

MAKE YOURSELF AT HOME.

A SHOWER?

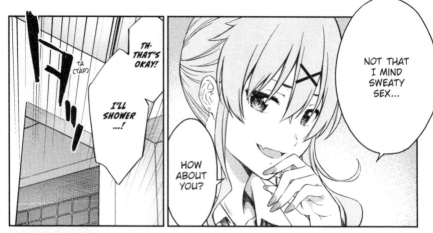

TH-THAT'S OKAY!

I'LL SHOWER....!

TA (TAP)

NOT THAT I MIND SWEATY SEX...

HOW ABOUT YOU?

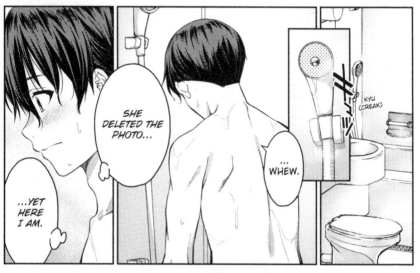

SHE DELETED THE PHOTO...

...YET HERE I AM.

... WHEW.

KYU (CREAK)

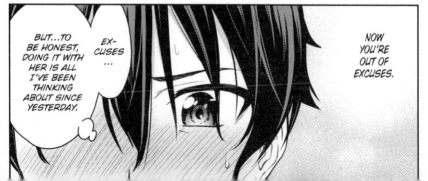

BUT...TO BE HONEST, DOING IT WITH HER IS ALL I'VE BEEN THINKING ABOUT SINCE YESTERDAY.

EX-CUSES...

NOW YOU'RE OUT OF EXCUSES.

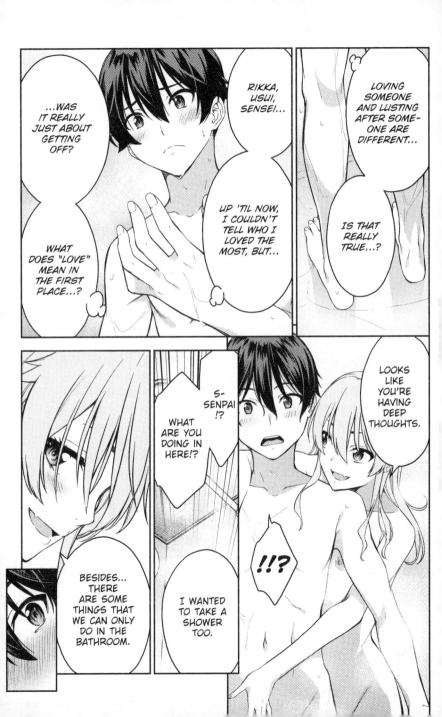

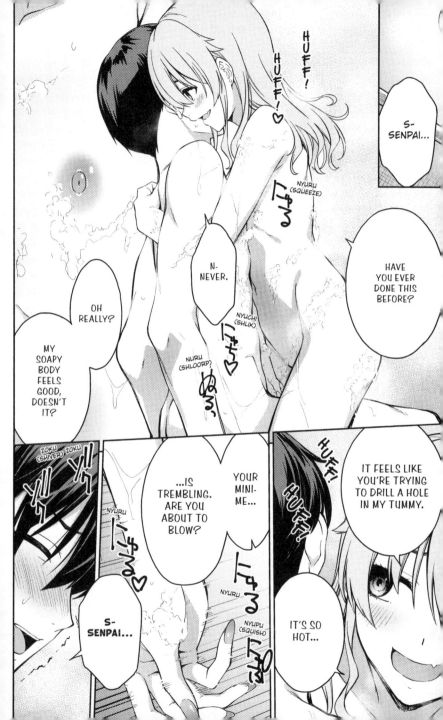

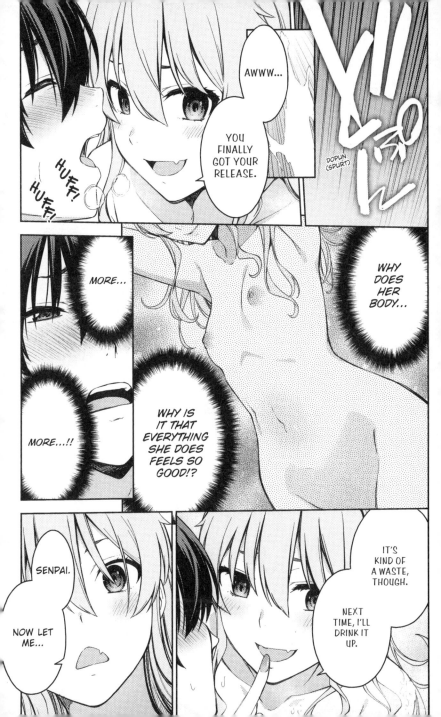

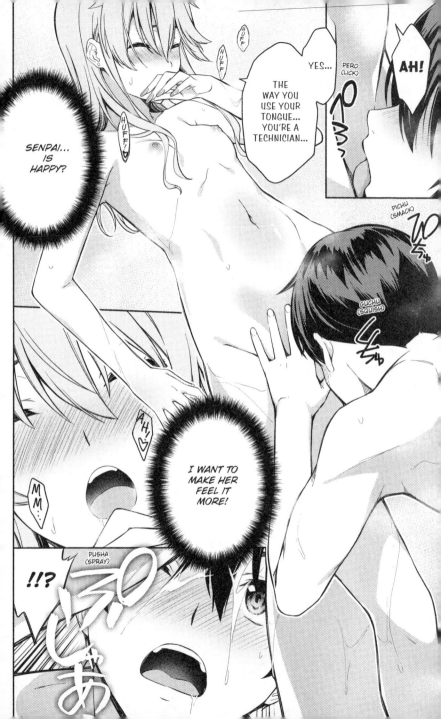

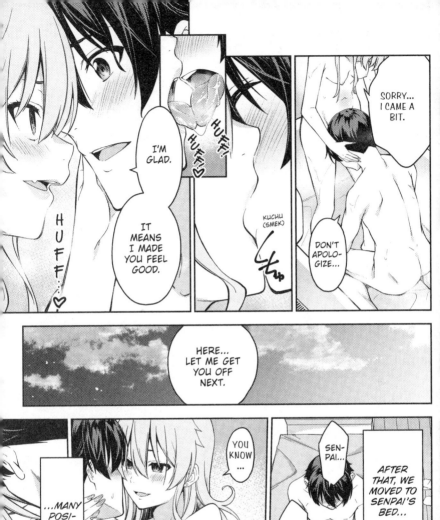

I'M GLAD.

HUFF!! HUFF!! ♥

IT MEANS I MADE YOU FEEL GOOD.

HUFF...♥

KUCHU (SMEK)

SORRY... I CAME A BIT.

DON'T APOLO-GIZE...

HERE... LET ME GET YOU OFF NEXT.

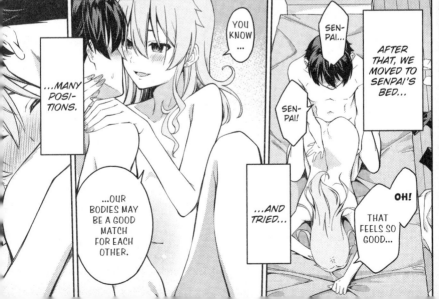

...MANY POSI-TIONS.

YOU KNOW...

...OUR BODIES MAY BE A GOOD MATCH FOR EACH OTHER.

SEN-PAI...

SEN-PAI!

AFTER THAT, WE MOVED TO SENPAI'S BED...

...AND TRIED...

OH! THAT FEELS SO GOOD...

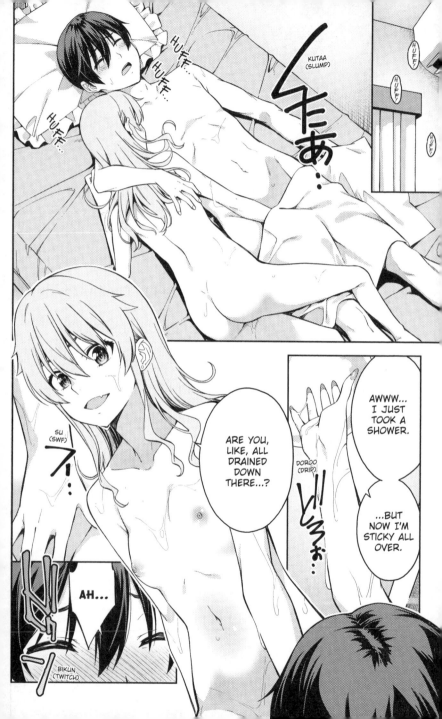

HUFF...

HUFF...

HUFF...

HUFF...

KUTAA
(SLUMP)

HUFF...

HUFF...

HUFF...

HUFF...

AWWW...
I JUST TOOK A
SHOWER.

...BUT
NOW I'M
STICKY ALL
OVER.

ARE YOU,
LIKE, ALL
DRAINED
DOWN
THERE...?

DOROO
(DRIP)

SU
(SWF)

AH...

BIKUN
(TWITCH)

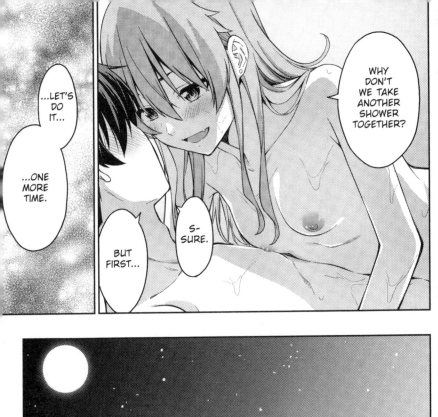

...LET'S DO IT...

...ONE MORE TIME.

WHY DON'T WE TAKE ANOTHER SHOWER TOGETHER?

BUT FIRST...

S-SURE.

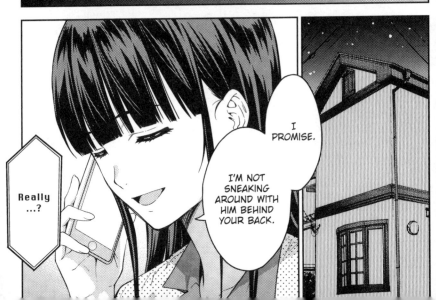

I PROMISE.

I'M NOT SNEAKING AROUND WITH HIM BEHIND YOUR BACK.

Really ...?

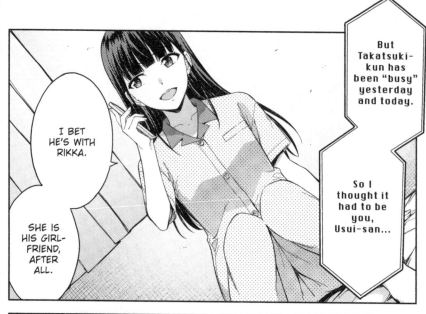

But Takatsuki-kun has been "busy" yesterday and today.

I BET HE'S WITH RIKKA.

SHE IS HIS GIRL-FRIEND, AFTER ALL.

So I thought it had to be you, Usui-san...

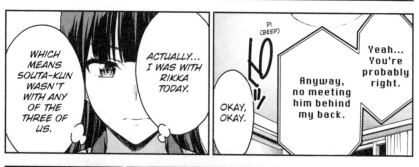

WHICH MEANS SOUTA-KUN WASN'T WITH ANY OF THE THREE OF US.

ACTUALLY... I WAS WITH RIKKA TODAY.

PI (BEEP)

OKAY, OKAY.

Anyway, no meeting him behind my back.

Yeah... You're probably right.

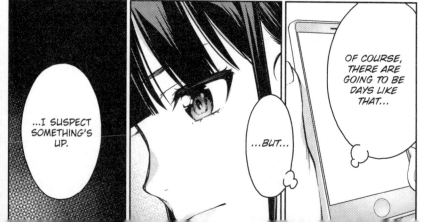

...I SUSPECT SOMETHING'S UP.

...BUT...

OF COURSE, THERE ARE GOING TO BE DAYS LIKE THAT...

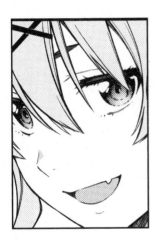

ZAWA (CHATTER)

ZAWA

ZAWA

DOYON (GLOOM)

...?

RIKKA!

WHAT'S WRONG?

TAKA-TSUKI-KUN!

GOOD MORNING.

DID YOU HAVE A FIGHT?

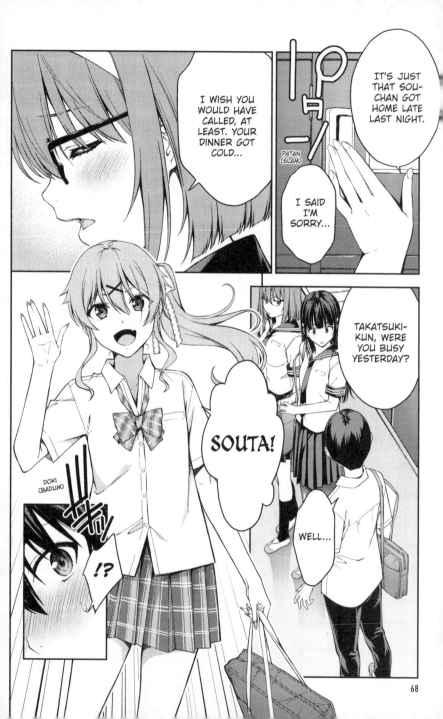

I WISH YOU WOULD HAVE CALLED, AT LEAST. YOUR DINNER GOT COLD...

IT'S JUST THAT SOU-CHAN GOT HOME LATE LAST NIGHT.

PATAN (SLAM)

I SAID I'M SORRY...

TAKATSUKI-KUN, WERE YOU BUSY YESTERDAY?

SOUTA!

DOKI (BADUM)

!?

WELL...

SOUTA-KUN AND NONOMIYA-SENPAI?

WHAT'S GOING ON...?

SEN-PAI...

CALLING ME "SOUTA" ISN'T—

WHAT'S WRONG WITH THAT? WE CERTAINLY KNOW EACH OTHER WELL ENOUGH NOW.

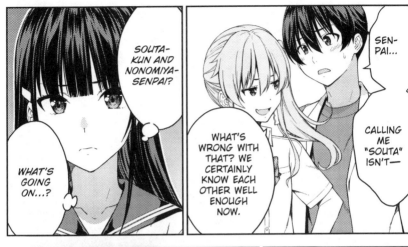

UM...

SHE'S MY GIRLFRIEND.

HUH...

SOUTA, WHO'S THIS?

IS SHE THE GIRL YOU MENTIONED YESTERDAY?

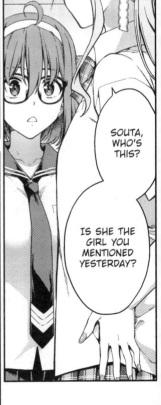

GREMORY TOLD ME HE HAD THREE WOMEN...

...BUT THIS MOUSY ONE IS THE GIRLFRIEND. GO FIGURE.

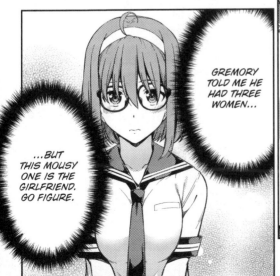

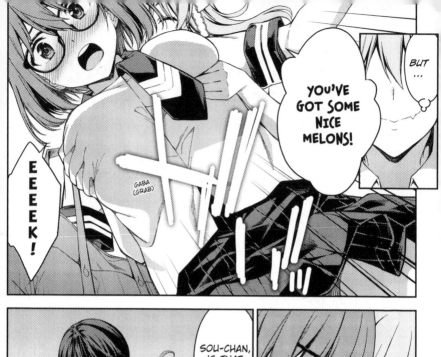

YOU'VE GOT SOME NICE MELONS!

BUT...

EEEEEK!

GABA (GRAB)

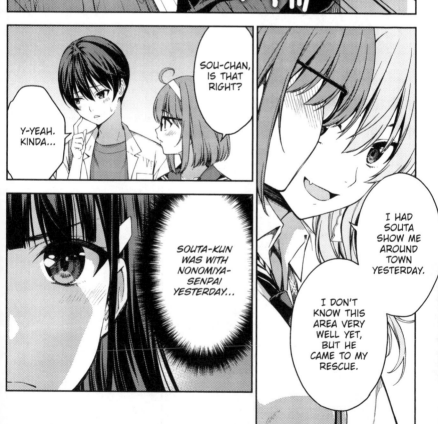

SOU-CHAN, IS THAT RIGHT?

Y-YEAH. KINDA...

SOUTA-KUN WAS WITH NONOMIYA-SENPAI YESTERDAY...

I HAD SOUTA SHOW ME AROUND TOWN YESTERDAY.

I DON'T KNOW THIS AREA VERY WELL YET, BUT HE CAME TO MY RESCUE.

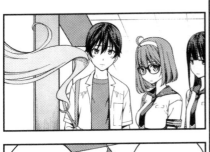

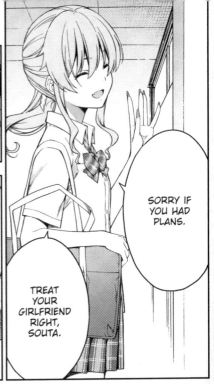

SORRY IF YOU HAD PLANS.

IF YOU'D EXPLAINED, I WOULDN'T HAVE GOTTEN MAD.

YOU SHOULD'VE JUST TOLD ME...

I'M SORRY...

TREAT YOUR GIRLFRIEND RIGHT, SOUTA.

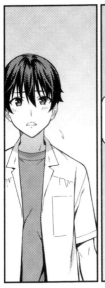

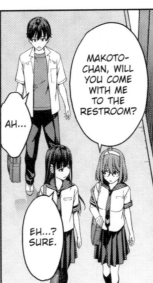

AH...

MAKOTO-CHAN, WILL YOU COME WITH ME TO THE RESTROOM?

EH...? SURE.

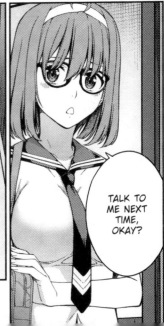

TALK TO ME NEXT TIME, OKAY?

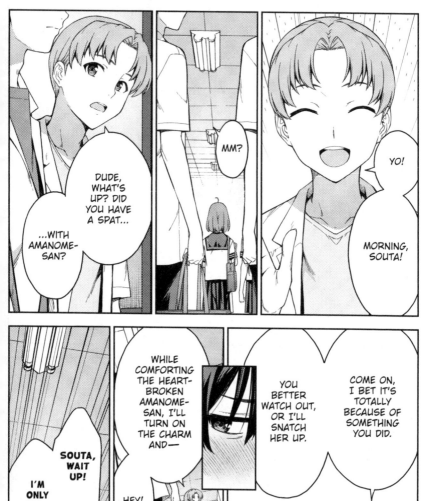

DUDE, WHAT'S UP? DID YOU HAVE A SPAT...

...WITH AMANOME-SAN?

MM?

YO!

MORNING, SOUTA!

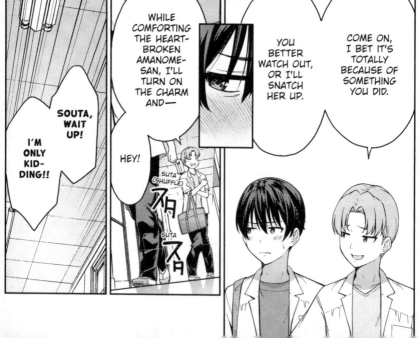

WHILE COMFORTING THE HEART-BROKEN AMANOME-SAN, I'LL TURN ON THE CHARM AND—

SOUTA, WAIT UP!

I'M ONLY KIDDING!!

HEY!

SUTA (SHUFFLE)

SUTA

YOU BETTER WATCH OUT, OR I'LL SNATCH HER UP.

COME ON, I BET IT'S TOTALLY BECAUSE OF SOMETHING YOU DID.

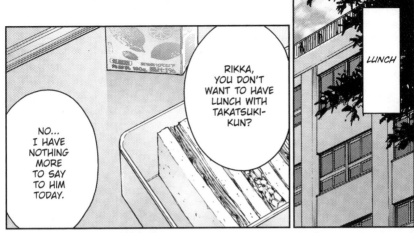

LUNCH

RIKKA, YOU DON'T WANT TO HAVE LUNCH WITH TAKATSUKI-KUN?

NO... I HAVE NOTHING MORE TO SAY TO HIM TODAY.

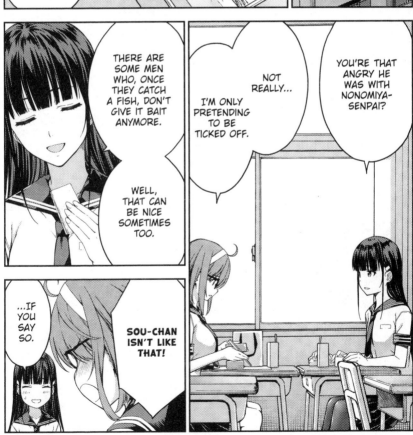

THERE ARE SOME MEN WHO, ONCE THEY CATCH A FISH, DON'T GIVE IT BAIT ANYMORE.

WELL, THAT CAN BE NICE SOMETIMES TOO.

NOT REALLY... I'M ONLY PRETENDING TO BE TICKED OFF.

YOU'RE THAT ANGRY HE WAS WITH NONOMIYA-SENPAI?

...IF YOU SAY SO.

SOU-CHAN ISN'T LIKE THAT!

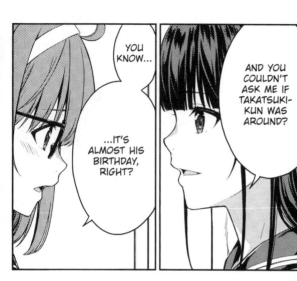
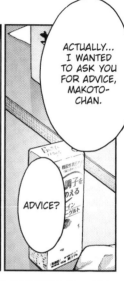

YOU KNOW...

...IT'S ALMOST HIS BIRTHDAY, RIGHT?

AND YOU COULDN'T ASK ME IF TAKATSUKI-KUN WAS AROUND?

ACTUALLY... I WANTED TO ASK YOU FOR ADVICE, MAKOTO-CHAN.

ADVICE?

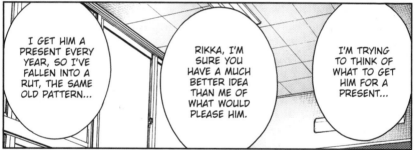

I GET HIM A PRESENT EVERY YEAR, SO I'VE FALLEN INTO A RUT, THE SAME OLD PATTERN...

RIKKA, I'M SURE YOU HAVE A MUCH BETTER IDEA THAN ME OF WHAT WOULD PLEASE HIM.

I'M TRYING TO THINK OF WHAT TO GET HIM FOR A PRESENT...

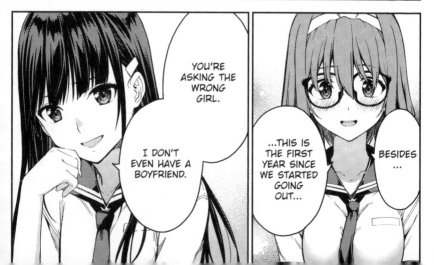

YOU'RE ASKING THE WRONG GIRL.

I DON'T EVEN HAVE A BOYFRIEND.

...THIS IS THE FIRST YEAR SINCE WE STARTED GOING OUT...

BESIDES...

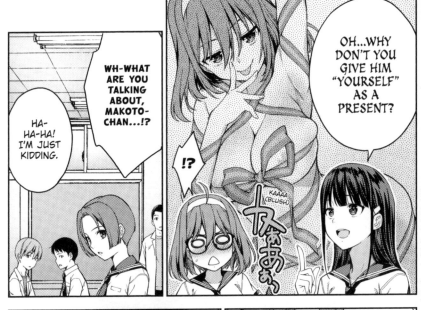

OH...WHY DON'T YOU GIVE HIM "YOURSELF" AS A PRESENT?

WH-WHAT ARE YOU TALKING ABOUT, MAKOTO-CHAN...!?

HA-HA-HA! I'M JUST KIDDING.

!?

KAAAA (BLUSH)

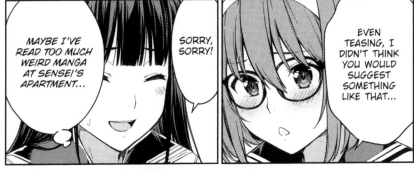

MAYBE I'VE READ TOO MUCH WEIRD MANGA AT SENSEI'S APARTMENT...

SORRY, SORRY!

EVEN TEASING, I DIDN'T THINK YOU WOULD SUGGEST SOMETHING LIKE THAT...

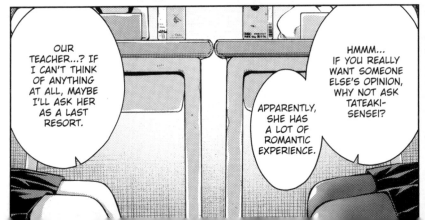

OUR TEACHER...? IF I CAN'T THINK OF ANYTHING AT ALL, MAYBE I'LL ASK HER AS A LAST RESORT.

HMMM... IF YOU REALLY WANT SOMEONE ELSE'S OPINION, WHY NOT ASK TATEAKI-SENSEI?

APPARENTLY, SHE HAS A LOT OF ROMANTIC EXPERIENCE.

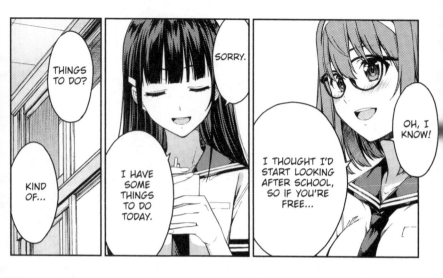

THINGS TO DO?

KIND OF...

SORRY.

I HAVE SOME THINGS TO DO TODAY.

OH, I KNOW!

I THOUGHT I'D START LOOKING AFTER SCHOOL, SO IF YOU'RE FREE...

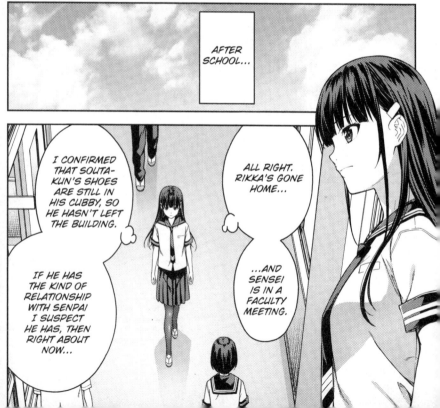

AFTER SCHOOL...

I CONFIRMED THAT SOUTA-KUN'S SHOES ARE STILL IN HIS CUBBY, SO HE HASN'T LEFT THE BUILDING.

IF HE HAS THE KIND OF RELATIONSHIP WITH SENPAI I SUSPECT HE HAS, THEN RIGHT ABOUT NOW...

ALL RIGHT. RIKKA'S GONE HOME...

...AND SENSEI IS IN A FACULTY MEETING.

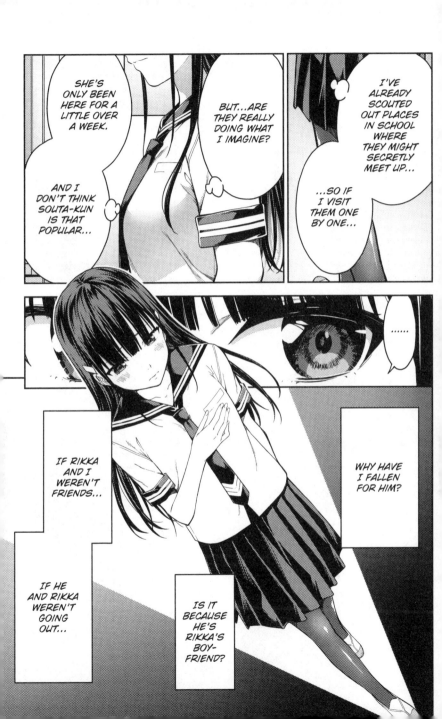

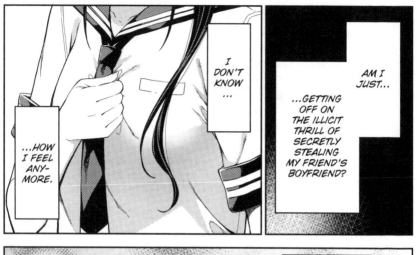

I DON'T KNOW...

...HOW I FEEL ANYMORE.

AM I JUST...

...GETTING OFF ON THE ILLICIT THRILL OF SECRETLY STEALING MY FRIEND'S BOYFRIEND?

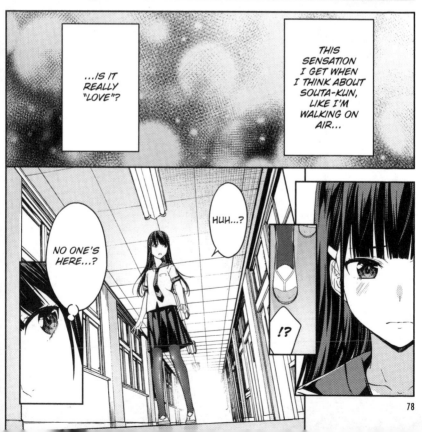

...IS IT REALLY "LOVE"?

THIS SENSATION I GET WHEN I THINK ABOUT SOUTA-KUN, LIKE I'M WALKING ON AIR...

NO ONE'S HERE...?

HUH...?

!?

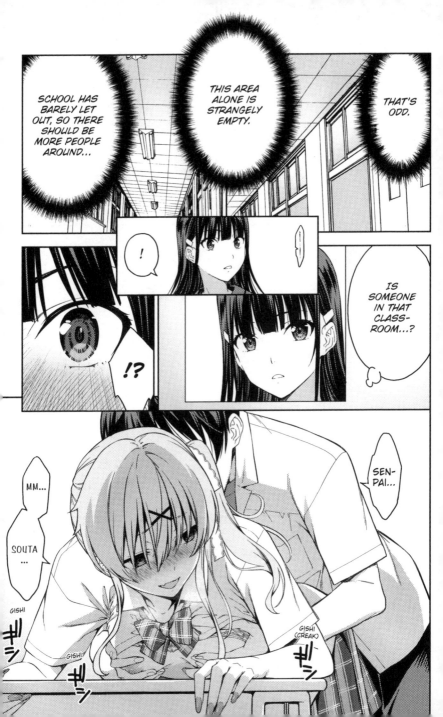

SCHOOL HAS BARELY LET OUT, SO THERE SHOULD BE MORE PEOPLE AROUND...

THIS AREA ALONE IS STRANGELY EMPTY.

THAT'S ODD.

!

IS SOMEONE IN THAT CLASS-ROOM...?

!?

MM...

SOUTA...

SEN-PAI...

GISHI

GISHI

GISHI (CREAK)

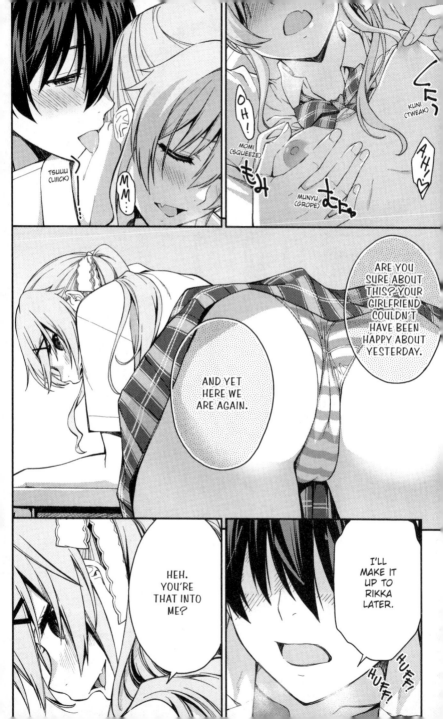

TSUUU
(LIIICK)

MM!

OH!

MOMI
(SQUEEZE)

MUNYU
(GROPE)

KUNI
(TWEAK)

AH!♥

ARE YOU SURE ABOUT THIS? YOUR GIRLFRIEND COULDN'T HAVE BEEN HAPPY ABOUT YESTERDAY.

AND YET HERE WE ARE AGAIN.

HEH. YOU'RE THAT INTO ME?

I'LL MAKE IT UP TO RIKKA LATER.

HUFF!

HUFF!

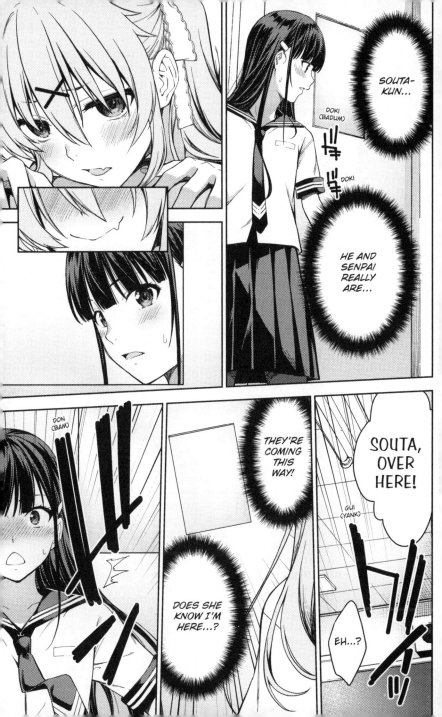

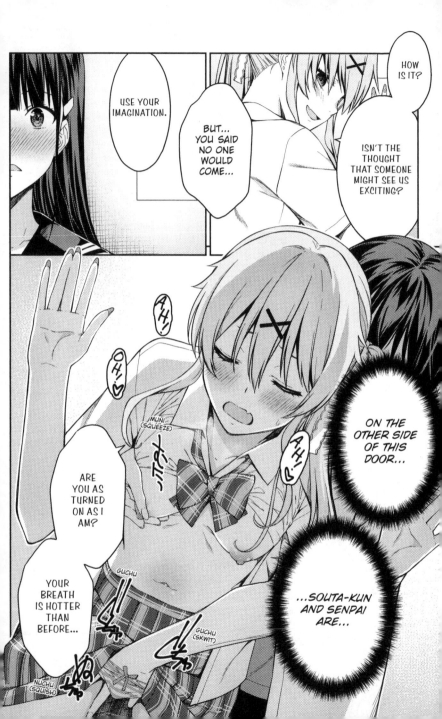

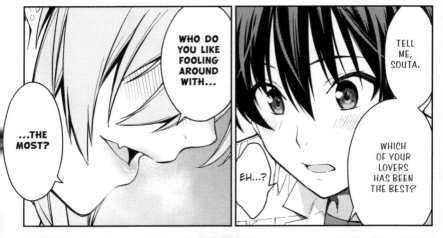

WHO DO YOU LIKE FOOLING AROUND WITH...

...THE MOST?

TELL ME, SOUTA.

EH...?

WHICH OF YOUR LOVERS HAS BEEN THE BEST?

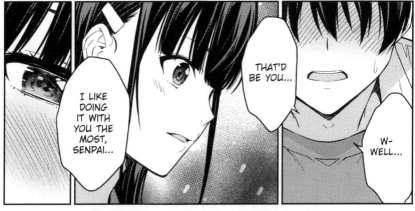

I LIKE DOING IT WITH YOU THE MOST, SENPAI...

THAT'D BE YOU...

W-WELL...

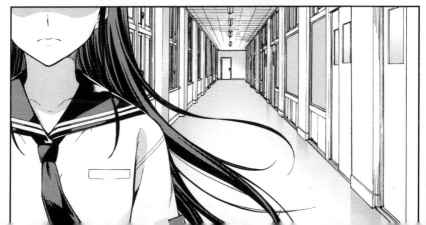

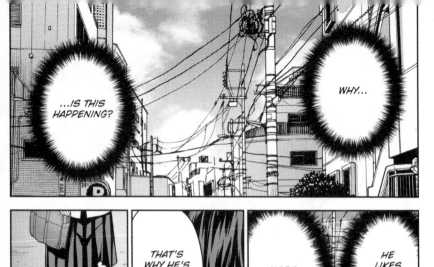

...IS THIS HAPPENING?

WHY...

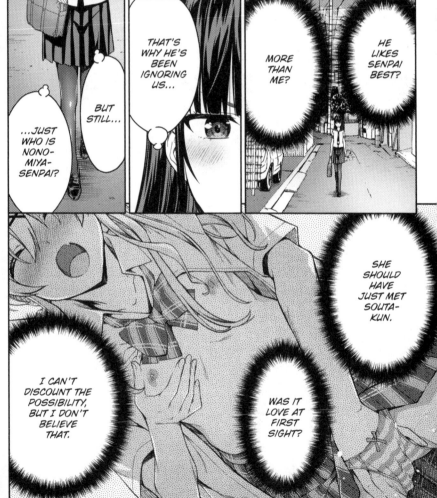

...JUST WHO IS NONO-MIYA-SENPAI?

BUT STILL...

THAT'S WHY HE'S BEEN IGNORING US...

MORE THAN ME?

HE LIKES SENPAI BEST?

SHE SHOULD HAVE JUST MET SOUTA-KUN.

I CAN'T DISCOUNT THE POSSIBILITY, BUT I DON'T BELIEVE THAT.

WAS IT LOVE AT FIRST SIGHT?

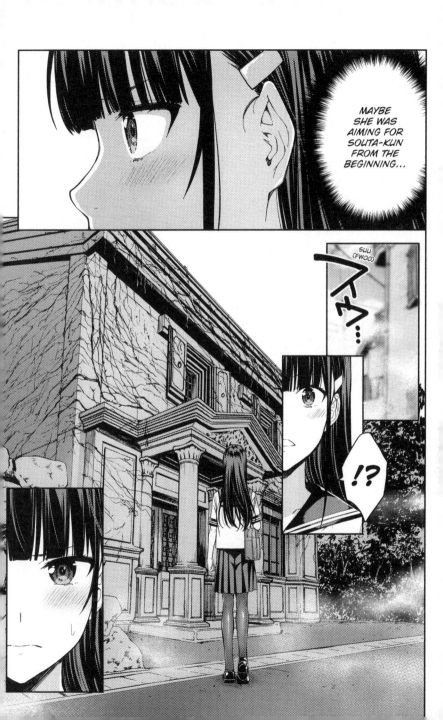

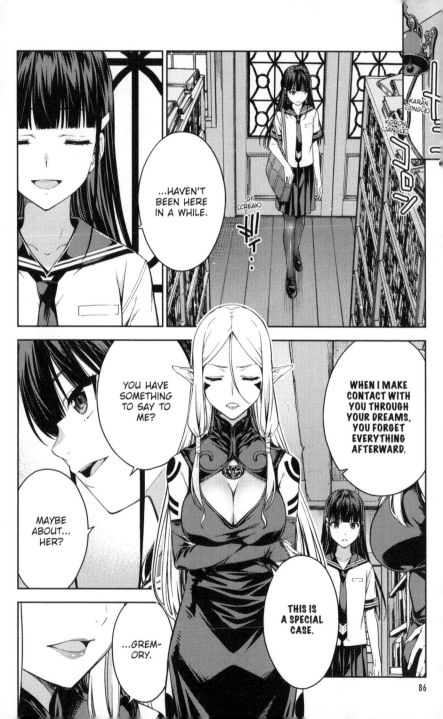

...HAVEN'T BEEN HERE IN A WHILE.

KARAN (JINGLE)

KORON (JINGLE)

GII (CREAK)

YOU HAVE SOMETHING TO SAY TO ME?

WHEN I MAKE CONTACT WITH YOU THROUGH YOUR DREAMS, YOU FORGET EVERYTHING AFTERWARD.

MAYBE ABOUT... HER?

...GREM- ORY.

THIS IS A SPECIAL CASE.

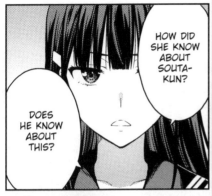

HOW DID SHE KNOW ABOUT SOUTA-KUN?

DOES HE KNOW ABOUT THIS?

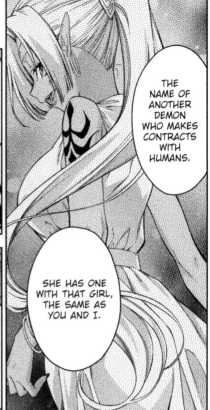

THE NAME OF ANOTHER DEMON WHO MAKES CONTRACTS WITH HUMANS.

SHE HAS ONE WITH THAT GIRL, THE SAME AS YOU AND I.

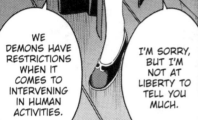

WE DEMONS HAVE RESTRICTIONS WHEN IT COMES TO INTERVENING IN HUMAN ACTIVITIES.

I'M SORRY, BUT I'M NOT AT LIBERTY TO TELL YOU MUCH.

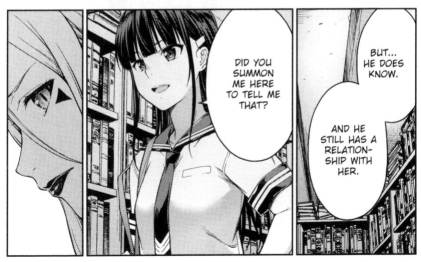

DID YOU SUMMON ME HERE TO TELL ME THAT?

BUT... HE DOES KNOW.

AND HE STILL HAS A RELATION-SHIP WITH HER.

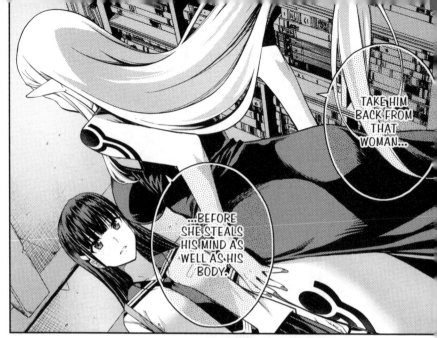

TAKE HIM BACK FROM THAT WOMAN...

...BEFORE SHE STEALS HIS MIND AS WELL AS HIS BODY.

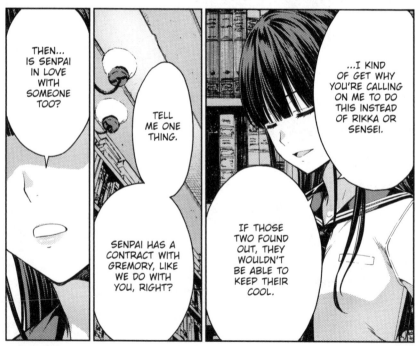

THEN... IS SENPAI IN LOVE WITH SOMEONE TOO?

TELL ME ONE THING.

SENPAI HAS A CONTRACT WITH GREMORY, LIKE WE DO WITH YOU, RIGHT?

...I KIND OF GET WHY YOU'RE CALLING ON ME TO DO THIS INSTEAD OF RIKKA OR SENSEI.

IF THOSE TWO FOUND OUT, THEY WOULDN'T BE ABLE TO KEEP THEIR COOL.

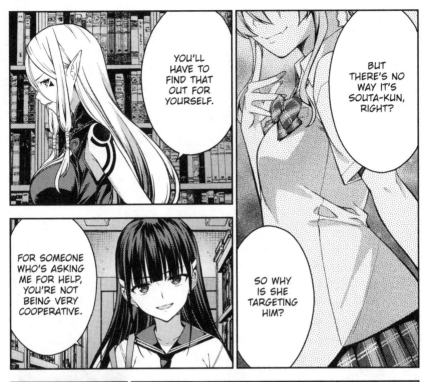

YOU'LL HAVE TO FIND THAT OUT FOR YOURSELF.

BUT THERE'S NO WAY IT'S SOUTA-KUN, RIGHT?

FOR SOMEONE WHO'S ASKING ME FOR HELP, YOU'RE NOT BEING VERY COOPERATIVE.

SO WHY IS SHE TARGETING HIM?

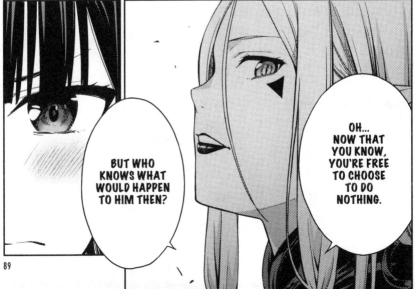

BUT WHO KNOWS WHAT WOULD HAPPEN TO HIM THEN?

OH... NOW THAT YOU KNOW, YOU'RE FREE TO CHOOSE TO DO NOTHING.

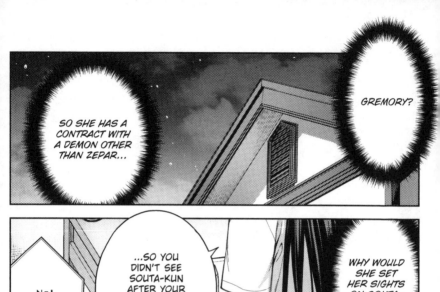

GREMORY?

SO SHE HAS A CONTRACT WITH A DEMON OTHER THAN ZEPAR...

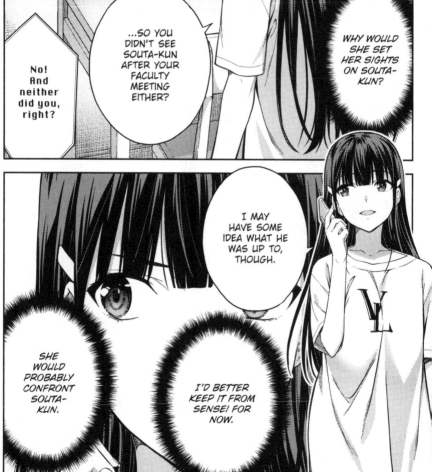

...SO YOU DIDN'T SEE SOUTA-KUN AFTER YOUR FACULTY MEETING EITHER?

No! And neither did you, right?

WHY WOULD SHE SET HER SIGHTS ON SOUTA-KUN?

I MAY HAVE SOME IDEA WHAT HE WAS UP TO, THOUGH.

SHE WOULD PROBABLY CONFRONT SOUTA-KUN.

I'D BETTER KEEP IT FROM SENSEI FOR NOW.

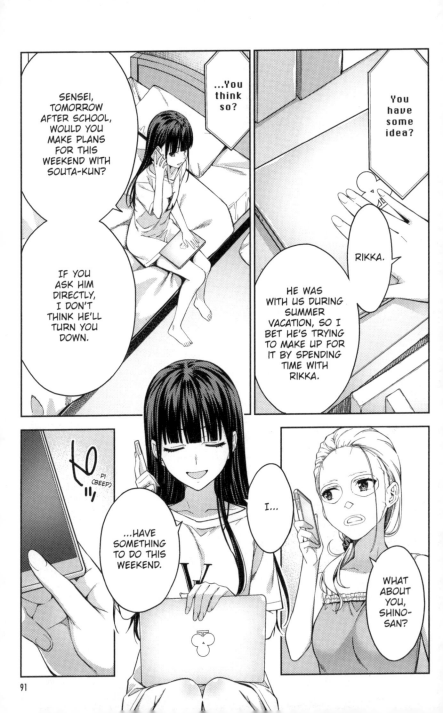

SENSEI, TOMORROW AFTER SCHOOL, WOULD YOU MAKE PLANS FOR THIS WEEKEND WITH SOUTA-KUN?

...YOU THINK SO?

YOU HAVE SOME IDEA?

IF YOU ASK HIM DIRECTLY, I DON'T THINK HE'LL TURN YOU DOWN.

RIKKA.

HE WAS WITH US DURING SUMMER VACATION, SO I BET HE'S TRYING TO MAKE UP FOR IT BY SPENDING TIME WITH RIKKA.

ピ
PI
(BEEP)

...HAVE SOMETHING TO DO THIS WEEKEND.

I...

WHAT ABOUT YOU, SHINO-SAN?

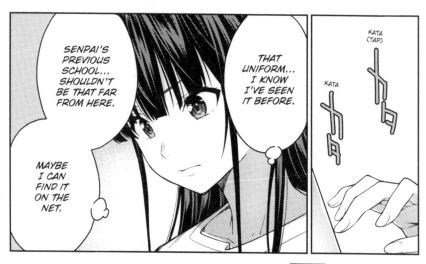

SENPAI'S PREVIOUS SCHOOL... SHOULDN'T BE THAT FAR FROM HERE.

MAYBE I CAN FIND IT ON THE NET.

THAT UNIFORM... I KNOW I'VE SEEN IT BEFORE.

KATA (TAP)

KATA

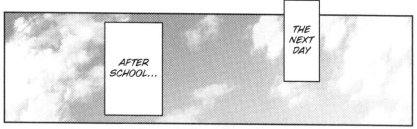

THE NEXT DAY

AFTER SCHOOL...

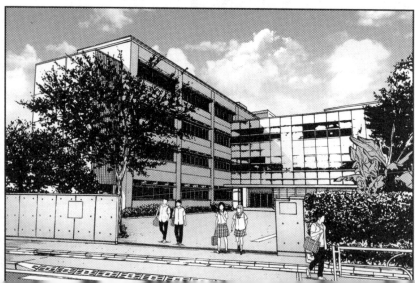

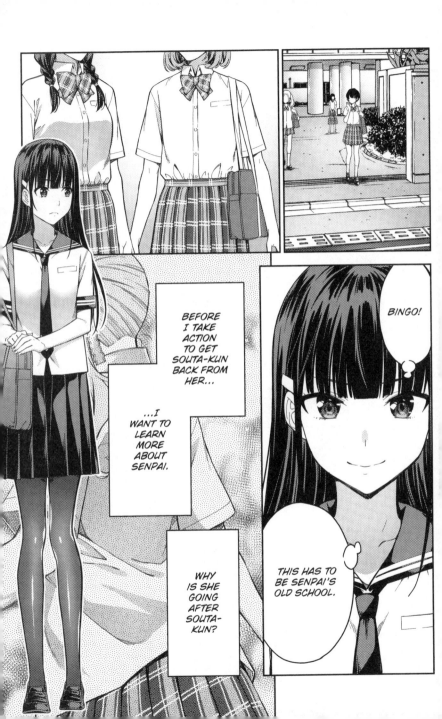

BEFORE I TAKE ACTION TO GET SOUTA-KUN BACK FROM HER...

...I WANT TO LEARN MORE ABOUT SENPAI.

BINGO!

THIS HAS TO BE SENPAI'S OLD SCHOOL.

WHY IS SHE GOING AFTER SOUTA-KUN?

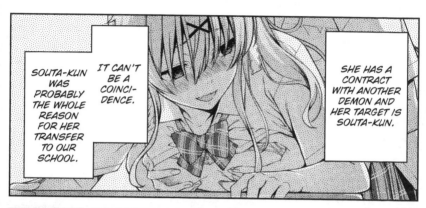

SOUTA-KUN WAS PROBABLY THE WHOLE REASON FOR HER TRANSFER TO OUR SCHOOL.

IT CAN'T BE A COINCIDENCE.

SHE HAS A CONTRACT WITH ANOTHER DEMON AND HER TARGET IS SOUTA-KUN.

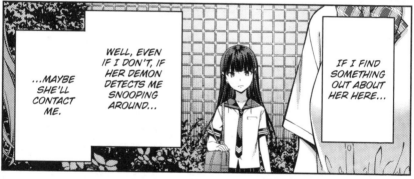

...MAYBE SHE'LL CONTACT ME.

WELL, EVEN IF I DON'T, IF HER DEMON DETECTS ME SNOOPING AROUND...

IF I FIND SOMETHING OUT ABOUT HER HERE...

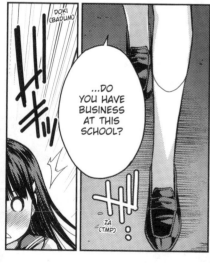

DOKI (BADUM)

...DO YOU HAVE BUSINESS AT THIS SCHOOL?

ZA (TMP)

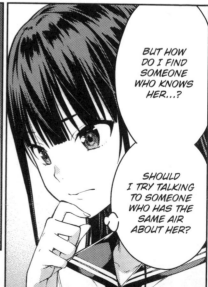

BUT HOW DO I FIND SOMEONE WHO KNOWS HER...?

SHOULD I TRY TALKING TO SOMEONE WHO HAS THE SAME AIR ABOUT HER?

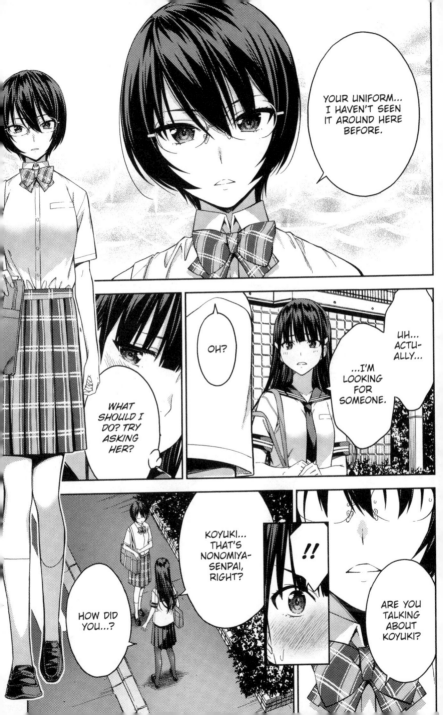

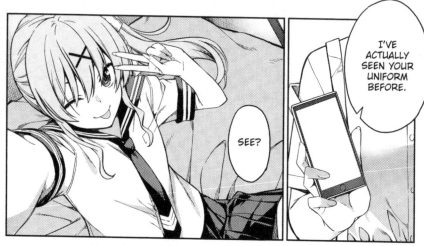

SEE?

I'VE ACTUALLY SEEN YOUR UNIFORM BEFORE.

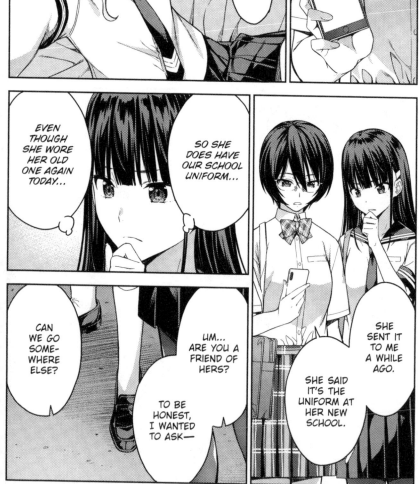

EVEN THOUGH SHE WORE HER OLD ONE AGAIN TODAY...

SO SHE DOES HAVE OUR SCHOOL UNIFORM...

CAN WE GO SOMEWHERE ELSE?

UM... ARE YOU A FRIEND OF HERS?

TO BE HONEST, I WANTED TO ASK—

SHE SENT IT TO ME A WHILE AGO.

SHE SAID IT'S THE UNIFORM AT HER NEW SCHOOL.

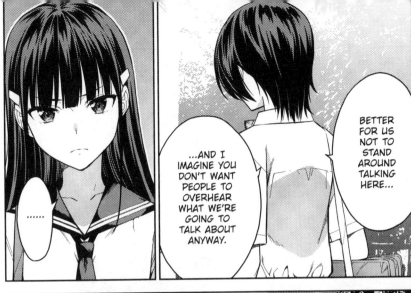

......

...AND I IMAGINE YOU DON'T WANT PEOPLE TO OVERHEAR WHAT WE'RE GOING TO TALK ABOUT ANYWAY.

BETTER FOR US NOT TO STAND AROUND TALKING HERE...

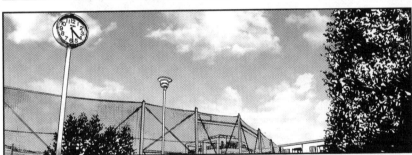

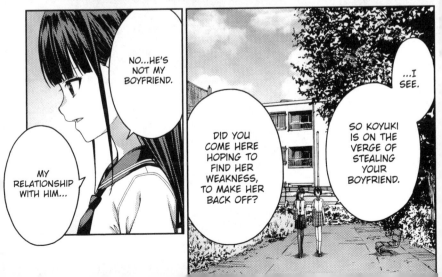

NO...HE'S NOT MY BOYFRIEND.

MY RELATIONSHIP WITH HIM...

...I SEE.

SO KOYUKI IS ON THE VERGE OF STEALING YOUR BOYFRIEND.

DID YOU COME HERE HOPING TO FIND HER WEAKNESS, TO MAKE HER BACK OFF?

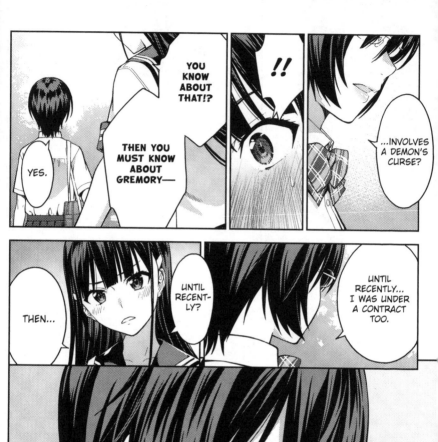

YOU KNOW ABOUT THAT!?

THEN YOU MUST KNOW ABOUT GREMORY—

YES.

!!

...INVOLVES A DEMON'S CURSE?

THEN...

UNTIL RECENT-LY?

UNTIL RECENTLY... I WAS UNDER A CONTRACT TOO.

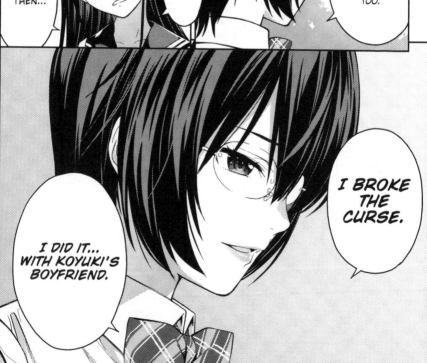

I DID IT... WITH KOYUKI'S BOYFRIEND.

I BROKE THE CURSE.

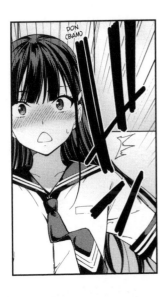

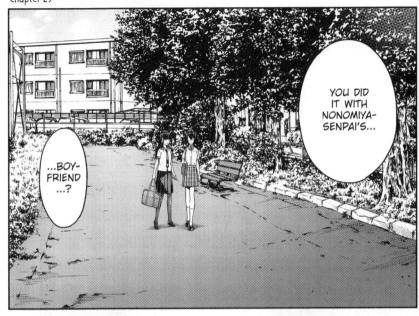

YOU DID IT WITH NONOMIYA-SENPAI'S...

...BOY-FRIEND...?

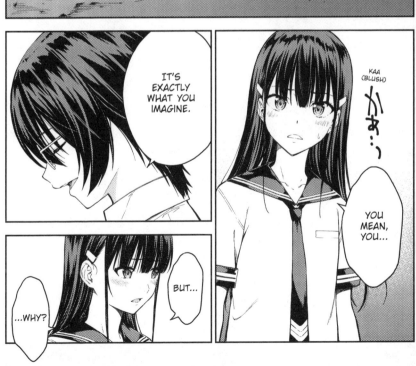

IT'S EXACTLY WHAT YOU IMAGINE.

KAA (BLUSH)

YOU MEAN, YOU...

...WHY?

BUT...

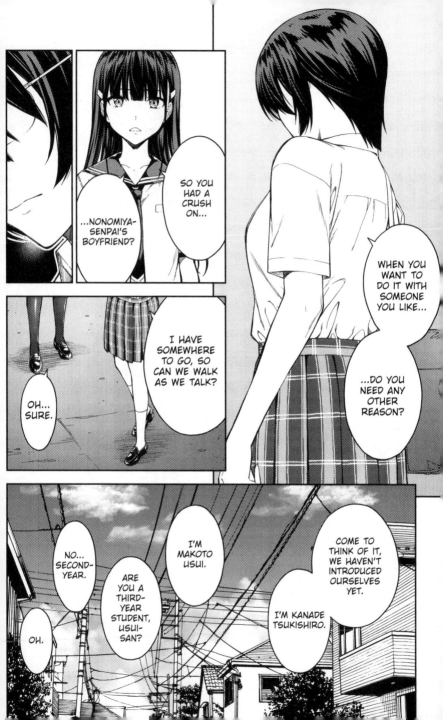

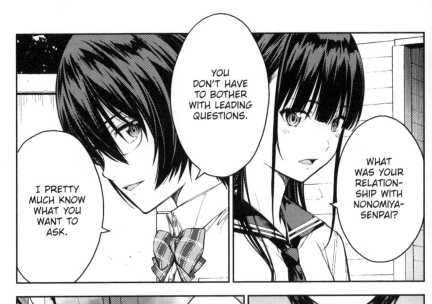

YOU DON'T HAVE TO BOTHER WITH LEADING QUESTIONS.

WHAT WAS YOUR RELATIONSHIP WITH NONOMIYA-SENPAI?

I PRETTY MUCH KNOW WHAT YOU WANT TO ASK.

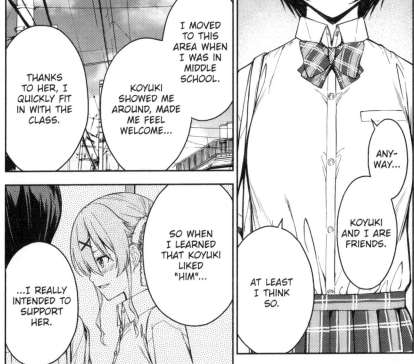

I MOVED TO THIS AREA WHEN I WAS IN MIDDLE SCHOOL.

THANKS TO HER, I QUICKLY FIT IN WITH THE CLASS.

KOYUKI SHOWED ME AROUND, MADE ME FEEL WELCOME...

ANYWAY...

KOYUKI AND I ARE FRIENDS.

SO WHEN I LEARNED THAT KOYUKI LIKED "HIM"...

...I REALLY INTENDED TO SUPPORT HER.

AT LEAST I THINK SO.

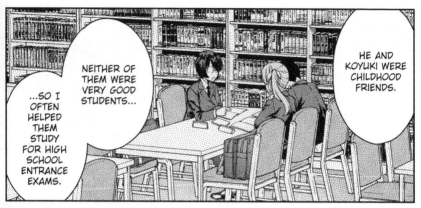

HE AND KOYUKI WERE CHILDHOOD FRIENDS.

NEITHER OF THEM WERE VERY GOOD STUDENTS...

...SO I OFTEN HELPED THEM STUDY FOR HIGH SCHOOL ENTRANCE EXAMS.

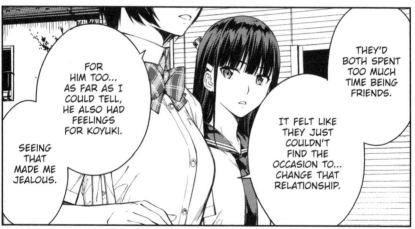

THEY'D BOTH SPENT TOO MUCH TIME BEING FRIENDS.

IT FELT LIKE THEY JUST COULDN'T FIND THE OCCASION TO... CHANGE THAT RELATIONSHIP.

FOR HIM TOO... AS FAR AS I COULD TELL, HE ALSO HAD FEELINGS FOR KOYUKI.

SEEING THAT MADE ME JEALOUS.

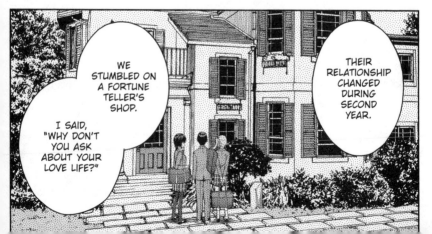

THEIR RELATIONSHIP CHANGED DURING SECOND YEAR.

WE STUMBLED ON A FORTUNE TELLER'S SHOP.

I SAID, "WHY DON'T YOU ASK ABOUT YOUR LOVE LIFE?"

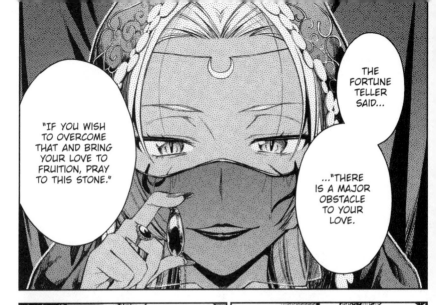

THE FORTUNE TELLER SAID...

..."THERE IS A MAJOR OBSTACLE TO YOUR LOVE.

"IF YOU WISH TO OVERCOME THAT AND BRING YOUR LOVE TO FRUITION, PRAY TO THIS STONE."

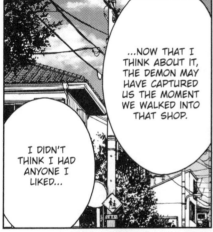

...NOW THAT I THINK ABOUT IT, THE DEMON MAY HAVE CAPTURED US THE MOMENT WE WALKED INTO THAT SHOP.

I DIDN'T THINK I HAD ANYONE I LIKED...

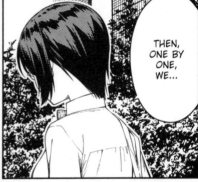

THEN, ONE BY ONE, WE...

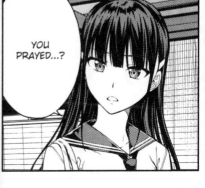

YOU PRAYED...?

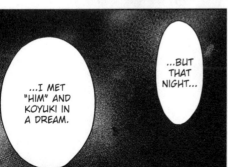

...I MET "HIM" AND KOYUKI IN A DREAM.

...BUT THAT NIGHT...

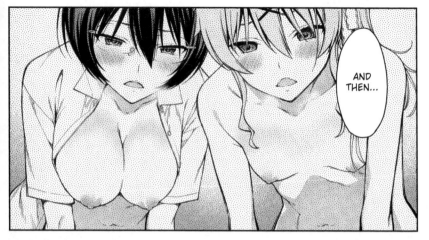

AND THEN...

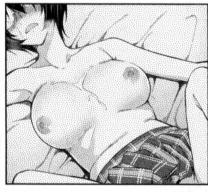

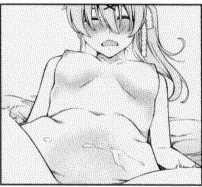

I'M SURE YOU KNOW WHAT HAPPENED AFTER THAT.

ACCORDING TO KOYUKI, YOUR CURSE AND OURS SEEM TO BE THE SAME.

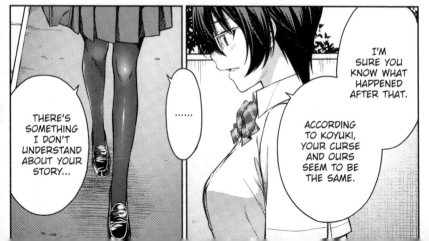

THERE'S SOMETHING I DON'T UNDERSTAND ABOUT YOUR STORY...

......

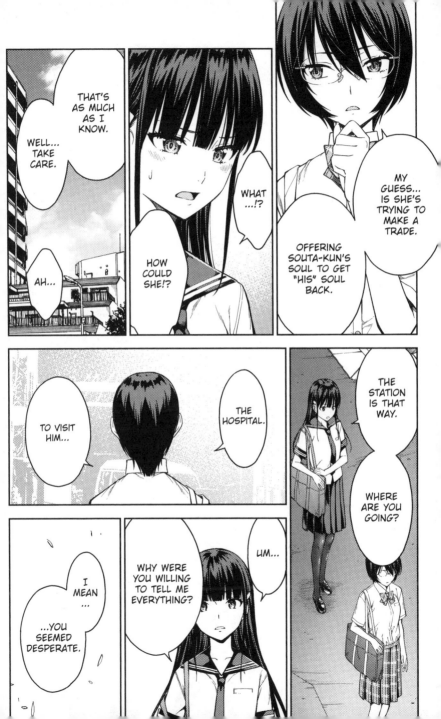

WELL... TAKE CARE.

THAT'S AS MUCH AS I KNOW.

AH...

HOW COULD SHE!?

WHAT ...!?

MY GUESS... IS SHE'S TRYING TO MAKE A TRADE.

OFFERING SOUTA-KUN'S SOUL TO GET "HIS" SOUL BACK.

TO VISIT HIM...

THE HOSPITAL.

THE STATION IS THAT WAY.

WHERE ARE YOU GOING?

I MEAN ...

...YOU SEEMED DESPERATE.

WHY WERE YOU WILLING TO TELL ME EVERYTHING?

UM...

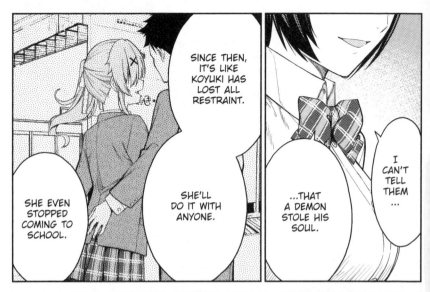

SINCE THEN, IT'S LIKE KOYUKI HAS LOST ALL RESTRAINT.

SHE'LL DO IT WITH ANYONE.

SHE EVEN STOPPED COMING TO SCHOOL.

...THAT A DEMON STOLE HIS SOUL.

I CAN'T TELL THEM...

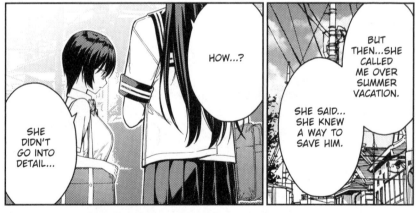

HOW...?

SHE DIDN'T GO INTO DETAIL...

BUT THEN...SHE CALLED ME OVER SUMMER VACATION.

SHE SAID... SHE KNEW A WAY TO SAVE HIM.

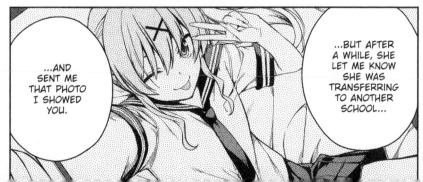

...AND SENT ME THAT PHOTO I SHOWED YOU.

...BUT AFTER A WHILE, SHE LET ME KNOW SHE WAS TRANSFERRING TO ANOTHER SCHOOL...

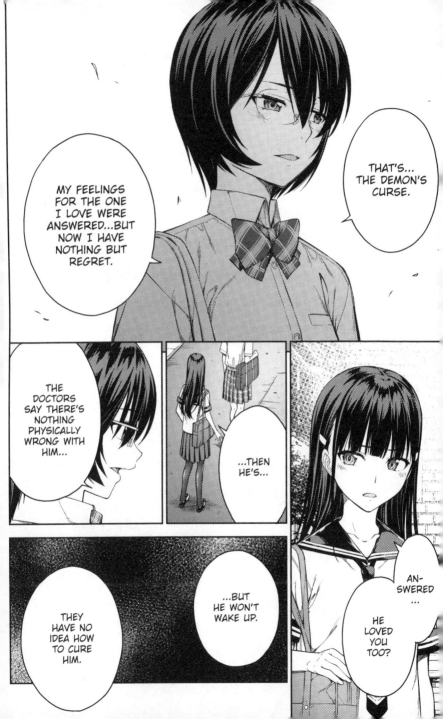

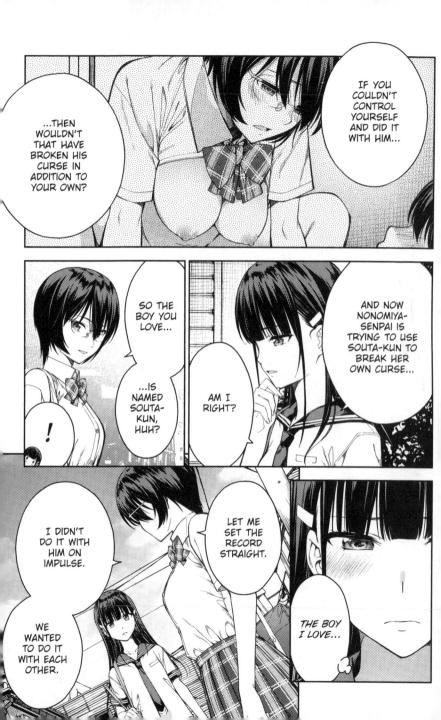

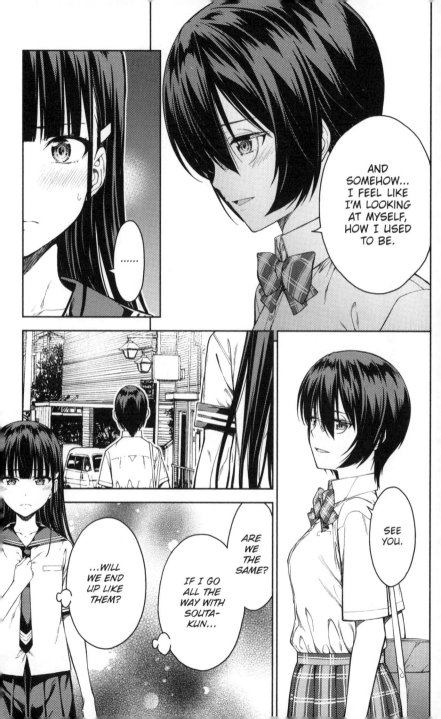

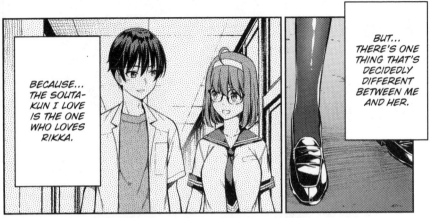

BECAUSE... THE SOUTA-KUN I LOVE IS THE ONE WHO LOVES RIKKA.

BUT... THERE'S ONE THING THAT'S DECIDEDLY DIFFERENT BETWEEN ME AND HER.

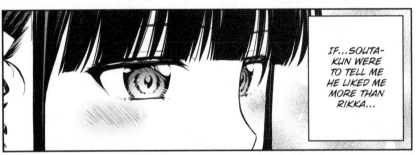

IF...SOUTA-KUN WERE TO TELL ME HE LIKED ME MORE THAN RIKKA...

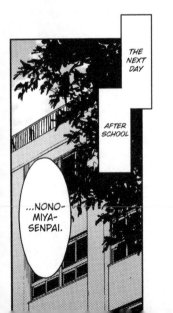

THE NEXT DAY

AFTER SCHOOL

...NONO-MIYA-SENPAI.

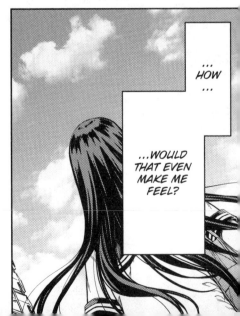

...HOW...

...WOULD THAT EVEN MAKE ME FEEL?

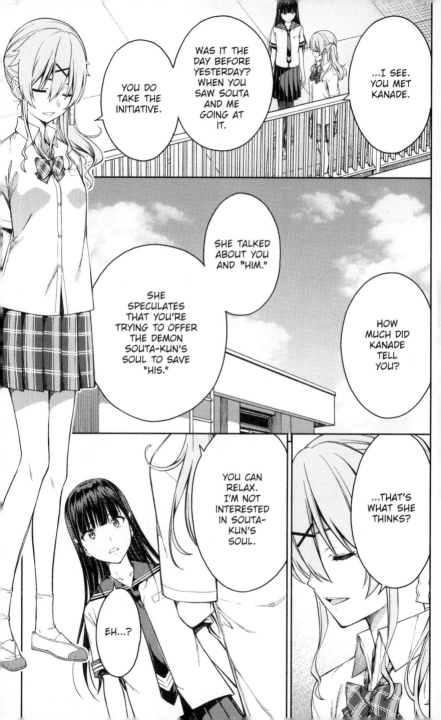

WAS IT THE DAY BEFORE YESTERDAY? WHEN YOU SAW SOUTA AND ME GOING AT IT.

YOU DO TAKE THE INITIATIVE.

...I SEE. YOU MET KANADE.

SHE TALKED ABOUT YOU AND "HIM."

SHE SPECULATES THAT YOU'RE TRYING TO OFFER THE DEMON SOUTA-KUN'S SOUL TO SAVE "HIS."

HOW MUCH DID KANADE TELL YOU?

YOU CAN RELAX. I'M NOT INTERESTED IN SOUTA-KUN'S SOUL.

...THAT'S WHAT SHE THINKS?

EH...?

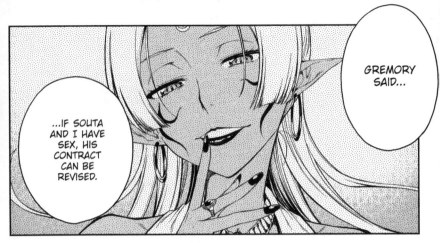

GREMORY SAID...

...IF SOUTA AND I HAVE SEX, HIS CONTRACT CAN BE REVISED.

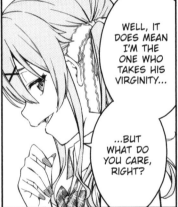

WELL, IT DOES MEAN I'M THE ONE WHO TAKES HIS VIRGINITY...

...BUT WHAT DO YOU CARE, RIGHT?

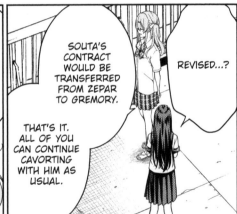

SOUTA'S CONTRACT WOULD BE TRANSFERRED FROM ZEPAR TO GREMORY.

THAT'S IT. ALL OF YOU CAN CONTINUE CAVORTING WITH HIM AS USUAL.

REVISED...?

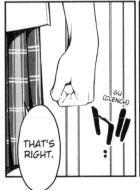

GU (CLENCH)

THAT'S RIGHT.

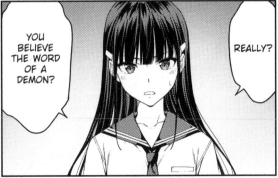

YOU BELIEVE THE WORD OF A DEMON?

REALLY?

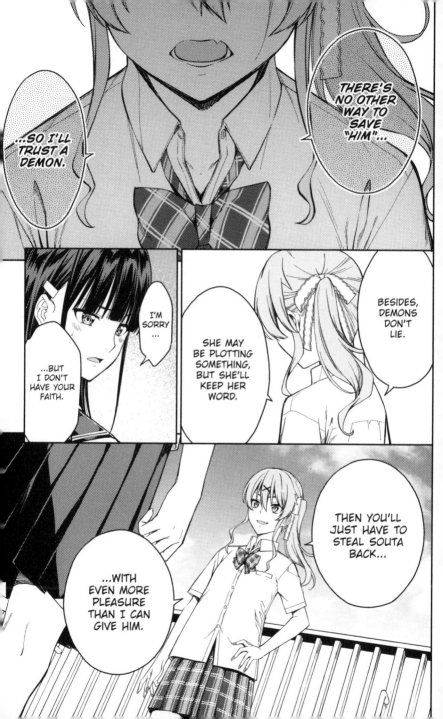

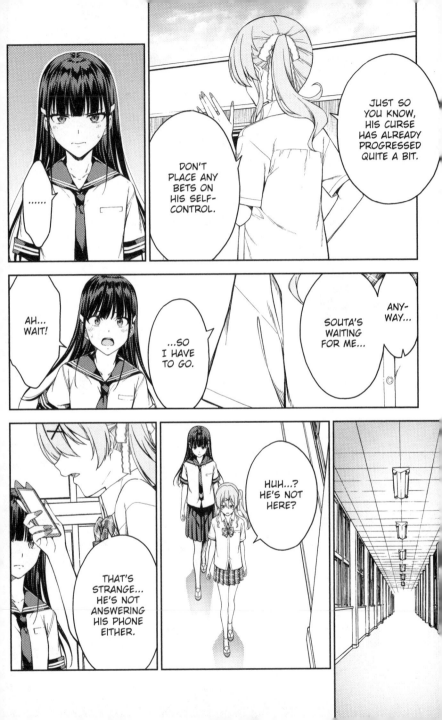

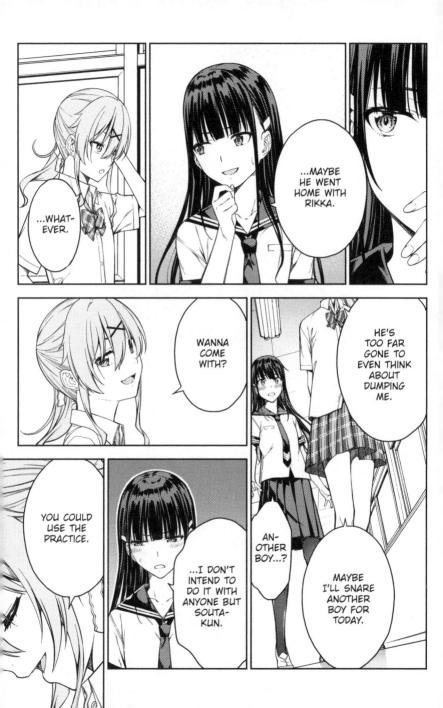

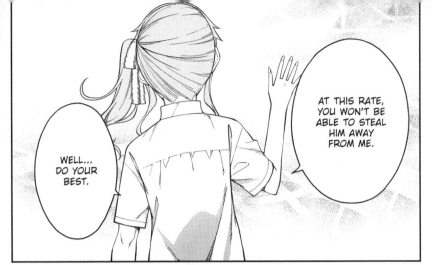

AT THIS RATE, YOU WON'T BE ABLE TO STEAL HIM AWAY FROM ME.

WELL... DO YOUR BEST.

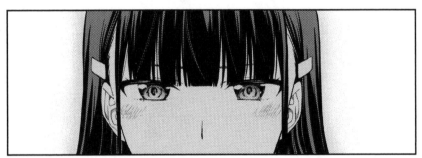

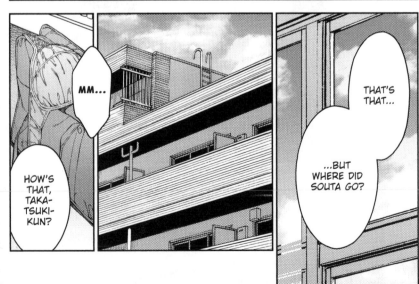

MM...

THAT'S THAT...

...BUT WHERE DID SOUTA GO?

HOW'S THAT, TAKA-TSUKI-KUN?

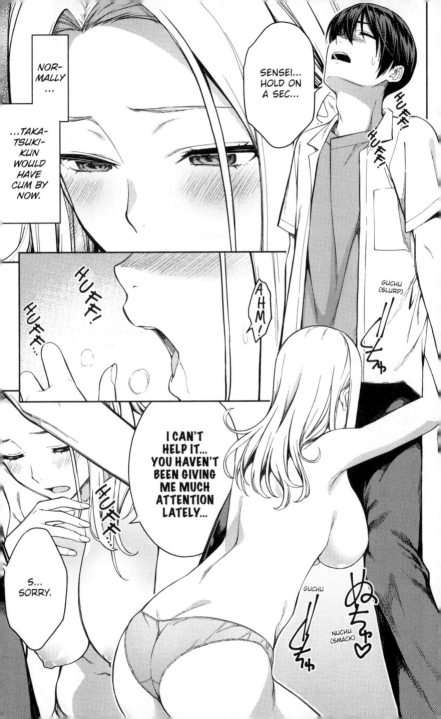

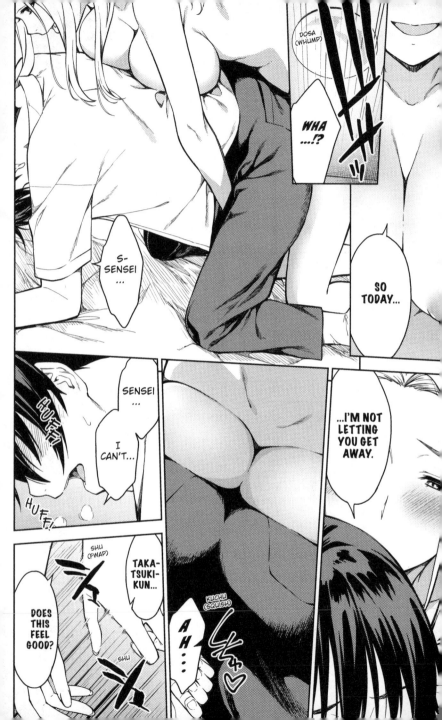

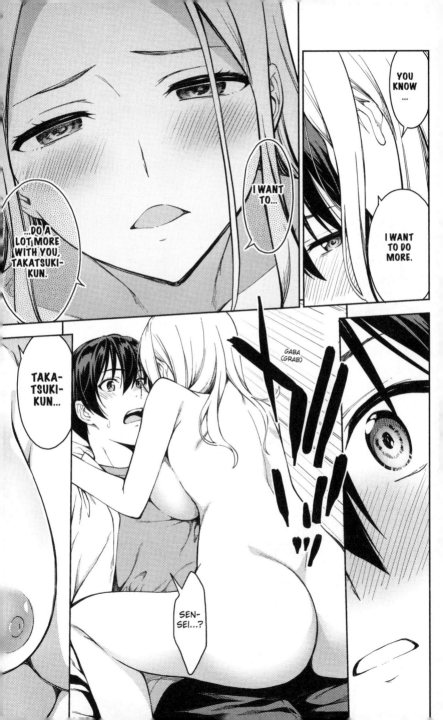

YOU KNOW...

I WANT TO...

I WANT TO DO MORE.

...DO A LOT MORE WITH YOU, TAKATSUKI-KUN.

GABA
(GRAB)

TAKATSUKI-KUN...

SEN-SEI...?

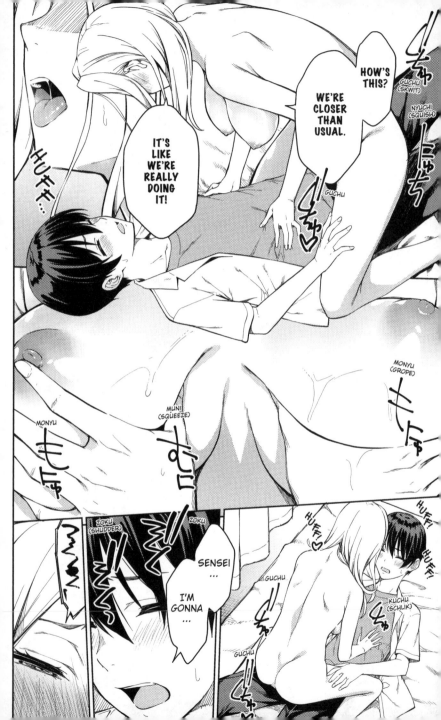

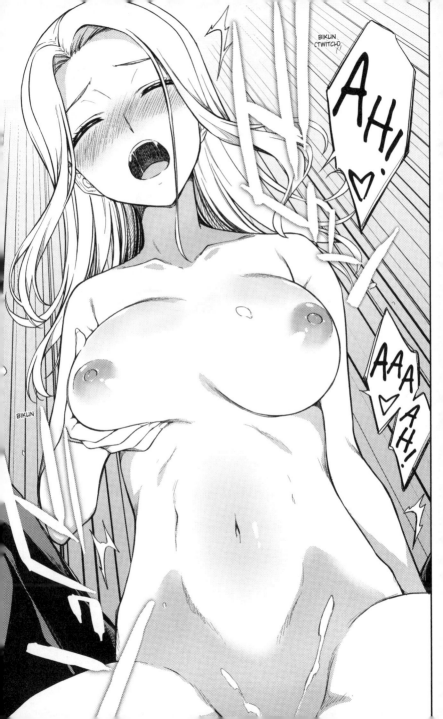

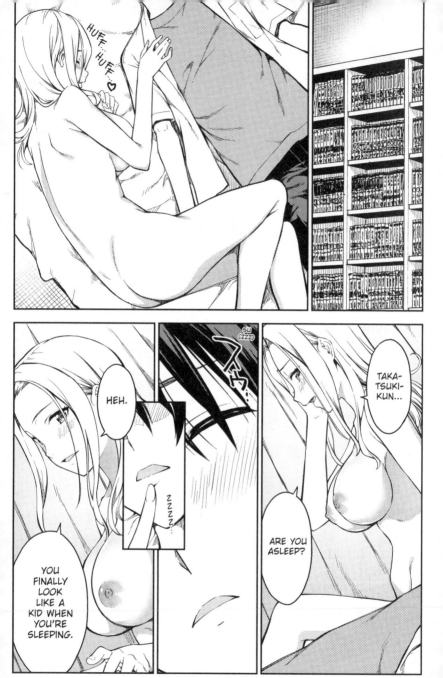

HUFF... HUFF...♡

HEH.

ZZZZ
ZZZZ...

TAKA-
TSUKI-
KUN...

ARE YOU
ASLEEP?

YOU
FINALLY
LOOK
LIKE A
KID WHEN
YOU'RE
SLEEPING.

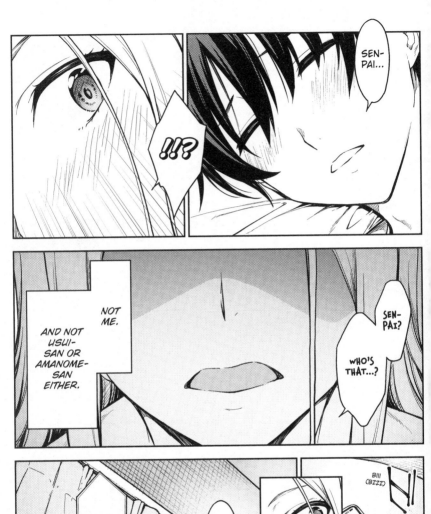

SEN-
PAI...

!!!?

NOT
ME.

AND NOT
USUI-
SAN OR
AMANOME-
SAN
EITHER.

SEN-
PAI?

WHO'S
THAT...?

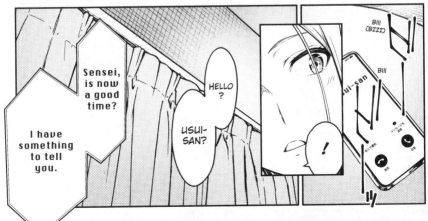

Sensei,
is now
a good
time?

I have
something
to tell
you.

HELLO
?

USUI-
SAN?

BIII
(BZZZ)

BIII

usui-san

!

!

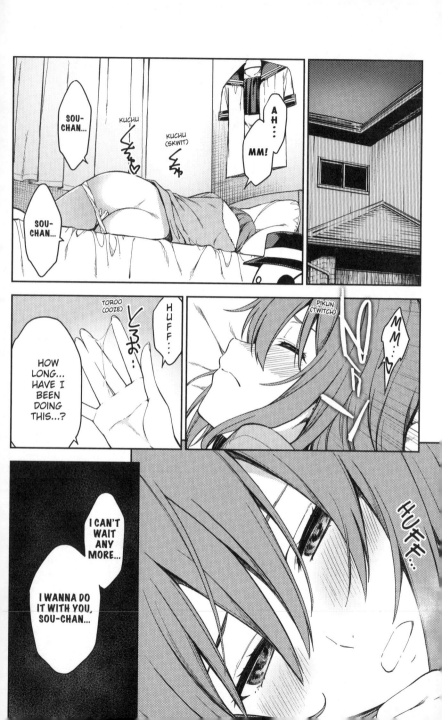

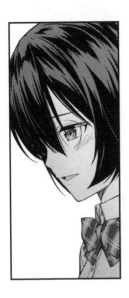

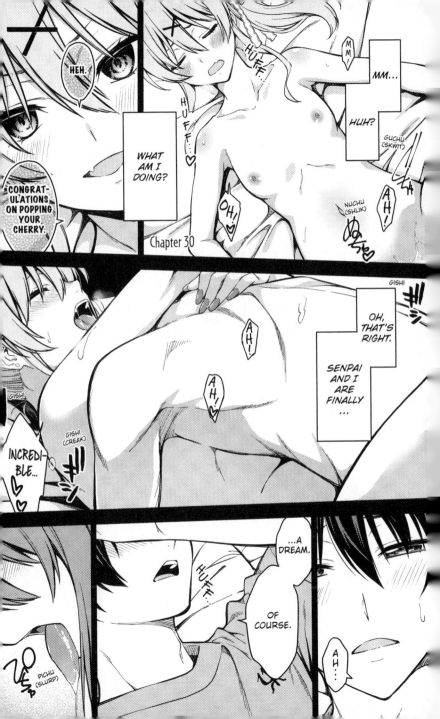

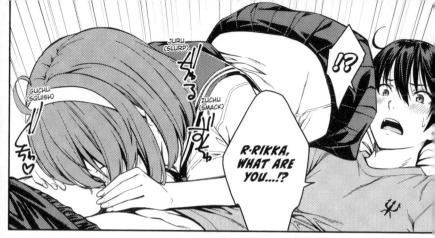

JURU (SLURP)

GUCHU (SQUISH)

ZUCHU (SMACK)

!?

R-RIKKA, WHAT ARE YOU....!?

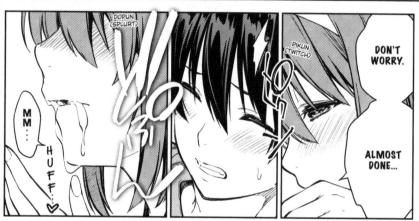

DOPUN (SPLURT)

PIKUN (TWITCH)

MM...

HUFF...♥

DON'T WORRY.

ALMOST DONE...

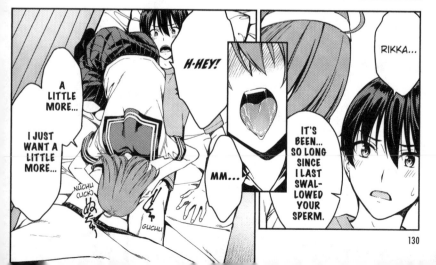

H-HEY!

A LITTLE MORE...

I JUST WANT A LITTLE MORE...

NUCHU (CLICK)

GUCHU

MM...

RIKKA...

IT'S BEEN... SO LONG SINCE I LAST SWALLOWED YOUR SPERM.

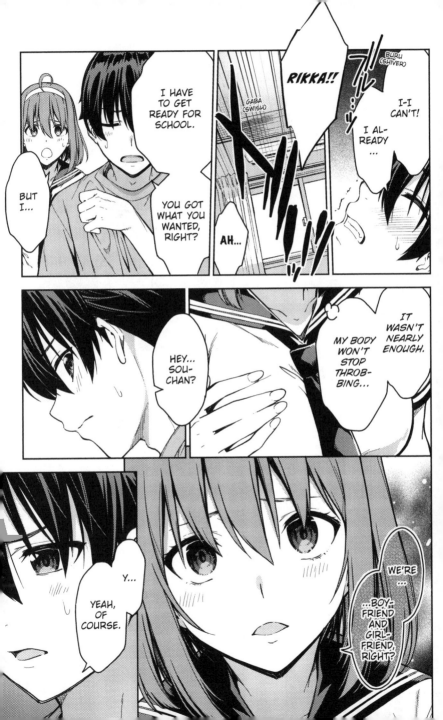

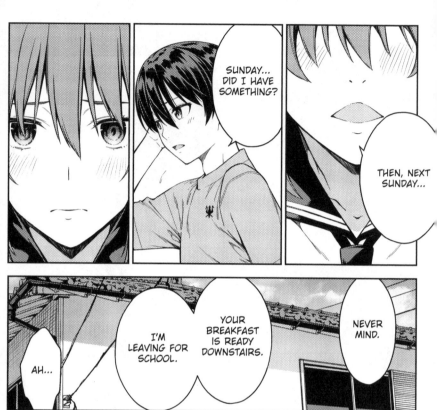

SUNDAY... DID I HAVE SOMETHING?

THEN, NEXT SUNDAY...

AH...

I'M LEAVING FOR SCHOOL.

YOUR BREAKFAST IS READY DOWNSTAIRS.

NEVER MIND.

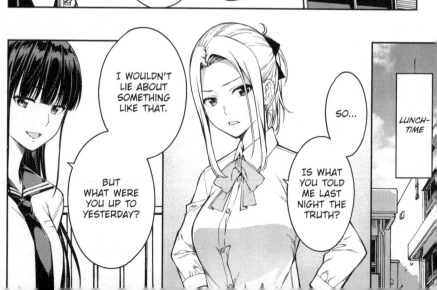

I WOULDN'T LIE ABOUT SOMETHING LIKE THAT.

BUT WHAT WERE YOU UP TO YESTERDAY?

SO...

IS WHAT YOU TOLD ME LAST NIGHT THE TRUTH?

LUNCH-TIME

NEXT TIME, I GET TO MONOPOLIZE SOUTA-KUN FOR A WHOLE DAY.

NOTHING SPECIAL.

UP TO...?

...I COULDN'T HELP MYSELF.

YOU'RE THE ONE WHO TOLD ME NOT TO GO SNEAKING AROUND BEHIND YOUR BACK.

...BUT IT'S HARD TO BELIEVE TAKATSUKI-KUN WOULD HAVE...

...THAT KIND OF RELATIONSHIP WITH HER.

I FEEL LIKE SHE WOULDN'T BE HIS TYPE TO BEGIN WITH.

WELL, RIGHT NOW WE'D BETTER THINK ABOUT NONOMIYA-SENPAI.

WELL, SHE IS CUTE.

AND SHE SPREADS HER LEGS QUITE EASILY.

MAYBE HE FELL IN LOVE WITH THAT COMBO?

KOYUKI NONOMIYA-SAN... SHE STANDS OUT, SO I KNOW HER NAME AND FACE...

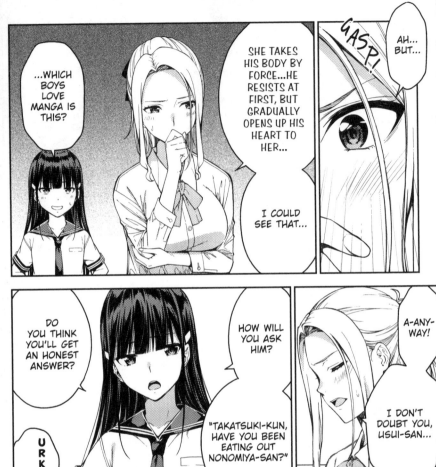

...WHICH BOYS LOVE MANGA IS THIS?

SHE TAKES HIS BODY BY FORCE...HE RESISTS AT FIRST, BUT GRADUALLY OPENS UP HIS HEART TO HER...

I COULD SEE THAT...

GASP!

AH... BUT...

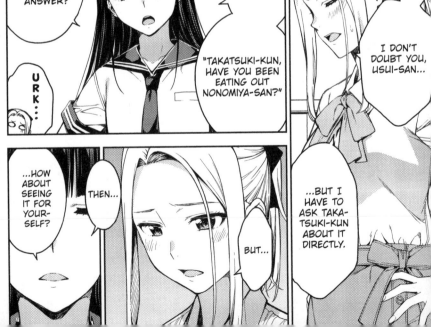

DO YOU THINK YOU'LL GET AN HONEST ANSWER?

HOW WILL YOU ASK HIM?

A-ANY-WAY!

I DON'T DOUBT YOU, USUI-SAN...

URK...

"TAKATSUKI-KUN, HAVE YOU BEEN EATING OUT NONOMIYA-SAN?"

...HOW ABOUT SEEING IT FOR YOUR-SELF?

THEN...

BUT...

...BUT I HAVE TO ASK TAKA-TSUKI-KUN ABOUT IT DIRECTLY.

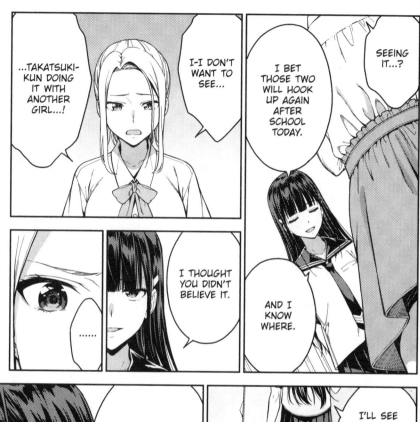

...TAKATSUKI-KUN DOING IT WITH ANOTHER GIRL...!

I-I DON'T WANT TO SEE...

I BET THOSE TWO WILL HOOK UP AGAIN AFTER SCHOOL TODAY.

SEEING IT...?

I THOUGHT YOU DIDN'T BELIEVE IT.

....

AND I KNOW WHERE.

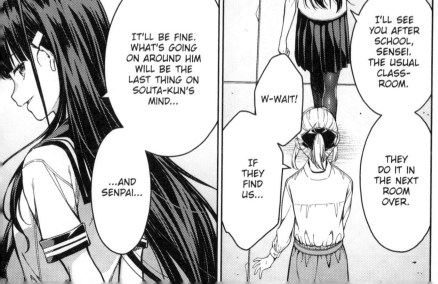

IT'LL BE FINE. WHAT'S GOING ON AROUND HIM WILL BE THE LAST THING ON SOUTA-KUN'S MIND...

...AND SENPAI...

W-WAIT!

IF THEY FIND US...

I'LL SEE YOU AFTER SCHOOL, SENSEI. THE USUAL CLASS-ROOM.

THEY DO IT IN THE NEXT ROOM OVER.

...ACTUALLY WANTS TO BE SEEN.

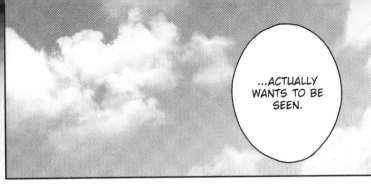

IT'S TRUE... I HAVEN'T BEEN SPENDING MUCH TIME WITH HER LATELY.

WE'RE BOYFRIEND AND GIRLFRIEND, RIGHT?

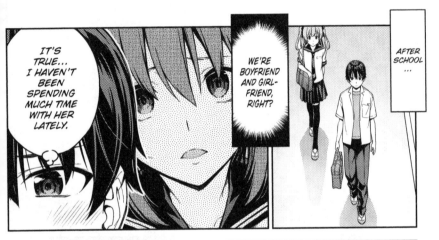

AFTER SCHOOL...

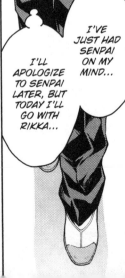

I'VE JUST HAD SENPAI ON MY MIND...

I'LL APOLOGIZE TO SENPAI LATER, BUT TODAY I'LL GO WITH RIKKA...

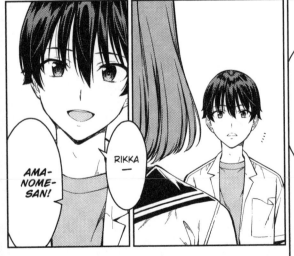

AMA-NOME-SAN!

RIKKA—

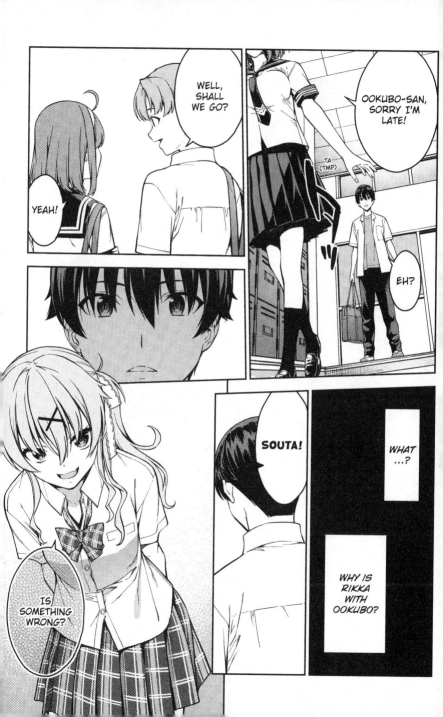

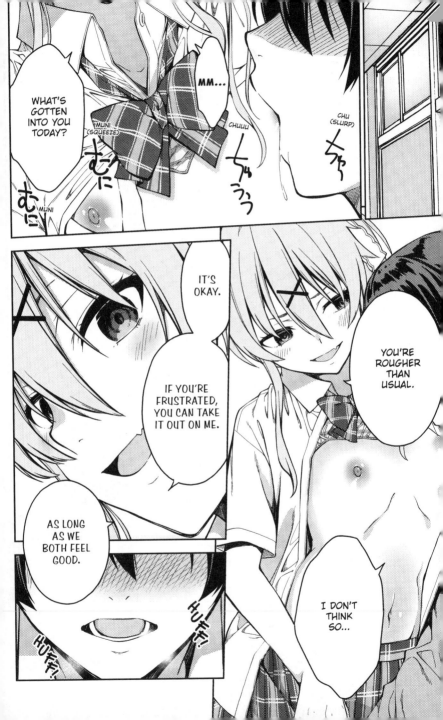

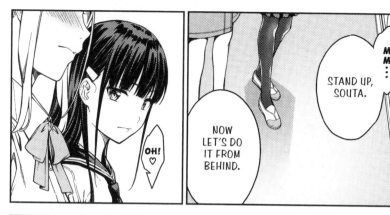

OH! ♡

NOW LET'S DO IT FROM BEHIND.

MM...

STAND UP, SOUTA.

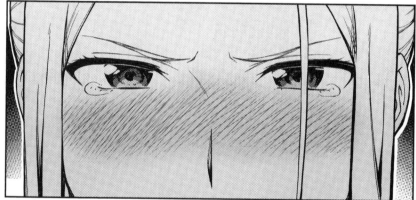

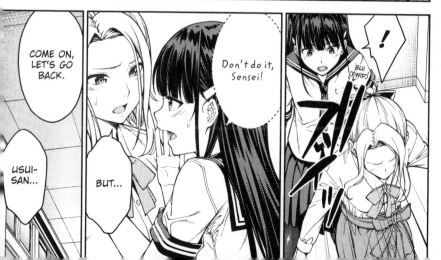

COME ON, LET'S GO BACK.

Don't do it, Sensei!

!

BUI (FWIP)

USUI-SAN...

BUT...

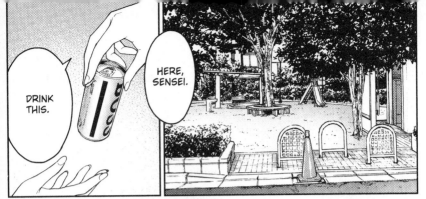

DRINK THIS.

HERE, SENSEI.

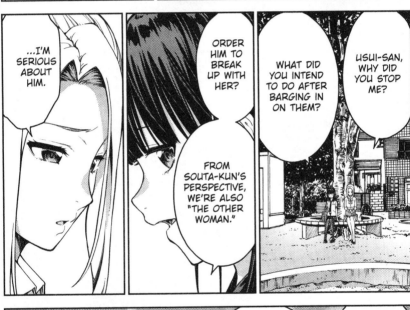

...I'M SERIOUS ABOUT HIM.

ORDER HIM TO BREAK UP WITH HER?

FROM SOUTA-KUN'S PERSPECTIVE, WE'RE ALSO "THE OTHER WOMAN."

WHAT DID YOU INTEND TO DO AFTER BARGING IN ON THEM?

USUI-SAN, WHY DID YOU STOP ME?

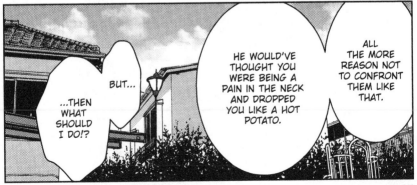

BUT...

...THEN WHAT SHOULD I DO!?

HE WOULD'VE THOUGHT YOU WERE BEING A PAIN IN THE NECK AND DROPPED YOU LIKE A HOT POTATO.

ALL THE MORE REASON NOT TO CONFRONT THEM LIKE THAT.

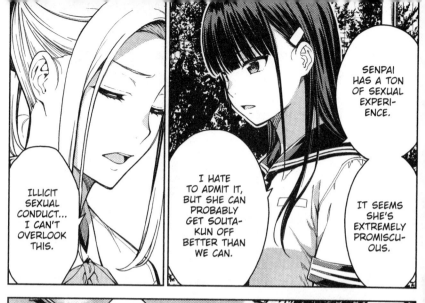

SENPAI HAS A TON OF SEXUAL EXPERIENCE.

IT SEEMS SHE'S EXTREMELY PROMISCUOUS.

I HATE TO ADMIT IT, BUT SHE CAN PROBABLY GET SOUTA-KUN OFF BETTER THAN WE CAN.

ILLICIT SEXUAL CONDUCT... I CAN'T OVERLOOK THIS.

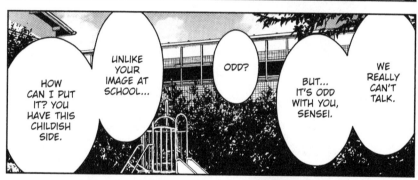

HOW CAN I PUT IT? YOU HAVE THIS CHILDISH SIDE.

UNLIKE YOUR IMAGE AT SCHOOL...

ODD?

BUT... IT'S ODD WITH YOU, SENSEI.

WE REALLY CAN'T TALK.

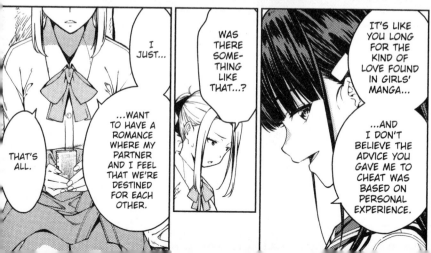

THAT'S ALL.

I JUST...

...WANT TO HAVE A ROMANCE WHERE MY PARTNER AND I FEEL THAT WE'RE DESTINED FOR EACH OTHER.

WAS THERE SOMETHING LIKE THAT...?

IT'S LIKE YOU LONG FOR THE KIND OF LOVE FOUND IN GIRLS' MANGA...

...AND I DON'T BELIEVE THE ADVICE YOU GAVE ME TO CHEAT WAS BASED ON PERSONAL EXPERIENCE.

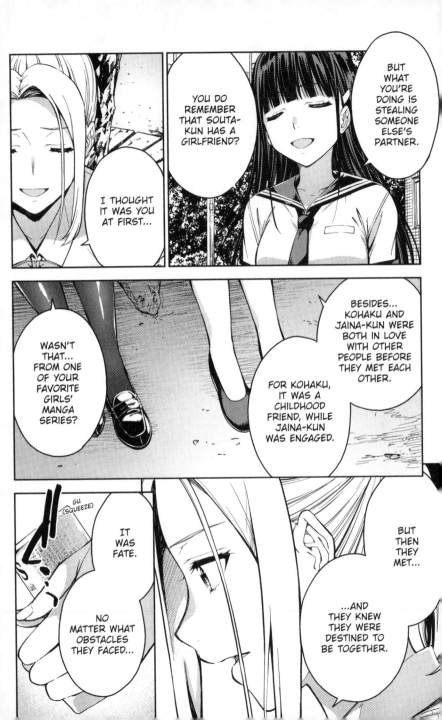

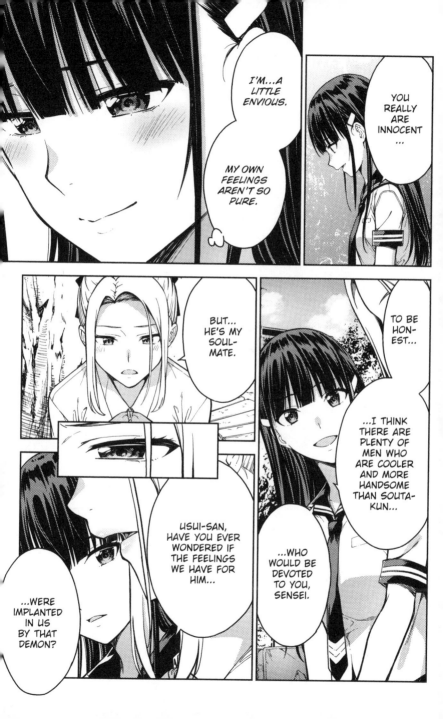

I'M...A LITTLE ENVIOUS.

MY OWN FEELINGS AREN'T SO PURE.

YOU REALLY ARE INNOCENT...

BUT... HE'S MY SOUL-MATE.

TO BE HON-EST...

...I THINK THERE ARE PLENTY OF MEN WHO ARE COOLER AND MORE HANDSOME THAN SOUTA-KUN...

USUI-SAN, HAVE YOU EVER WONDERED IF THE FEELINGS WE HAVE FOR HIM...

...WHO WOULD BE DEVOTED TO YOU, SENSEI.

...WERE IMPLANTED IN US BY THAT DEMON?

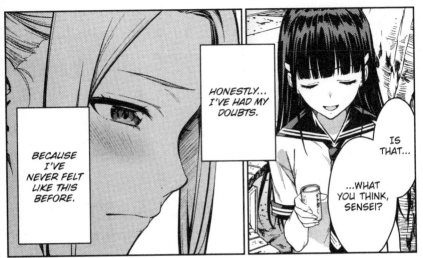

BECAUSE I'VE NEVER FELT LIKE THIS BEFORE.

HONESTLY... I'VE HAD MY DOUBTS.

IS THAT...

...WHAT YOU THINK, SENSEI?

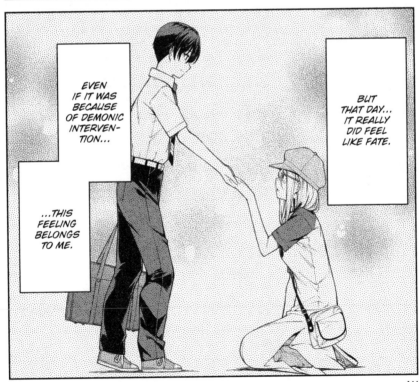

EVEN IF IT WAS BECAUSE OF DEMONIC INTERVENTION...

...THIS FEELING BELONGS TO ME.

BUT THAT DAY... IT REALLY DID FEEL LIKE FATE.

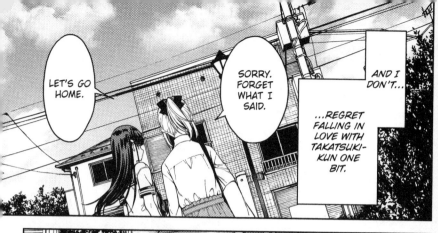

LET'S GO HOME.

SORRY. FORGET WHAT I SAID.

AND I DON'T...

...REGRET FALLING IN LOVE WITH TAKATSUKI-KUN ONE BIT.

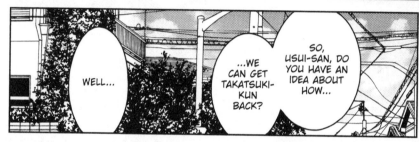

WELL...

...WE CAN GET TAKATSUKI-KUN BACK?

SO, USUI-SAN, DO YOU HAVE AN IDEA ABOUT HOW...

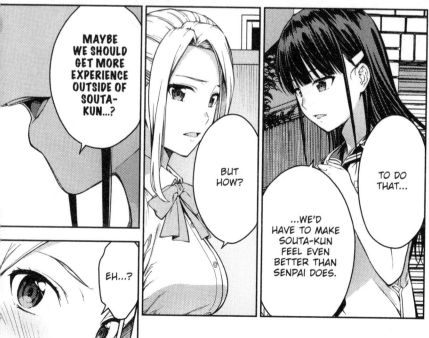

MAYBE WE SHOULD GET MORE EXPERIENCE OUTSIDE OF SOUTA-KUN...?

BUT HOW?

TO DO THAT...

...WE'D HAVE TO MAKE SOUTA-KUN FEEL EVEN BETTER THAN SENPAI DOES.

EH...?

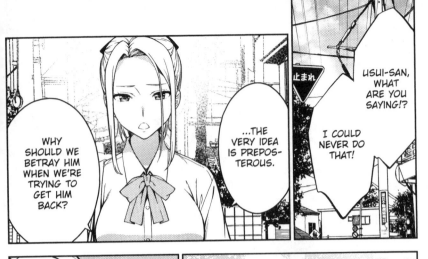

WHY SHOULD WE BETRAY HIM WHEN WE'RE TRYING TO GET HIM BACK?

...THE VERY IDEA IS PREPOSTEROUS.

USUI-SAN, WHAT ARE YOU SAYING!?

I COULD NEVER DO THAT!

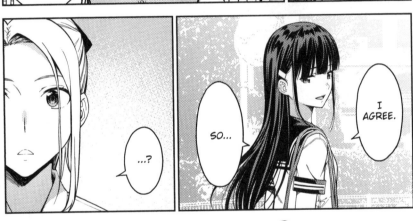

...?

SO...

I AGREE.

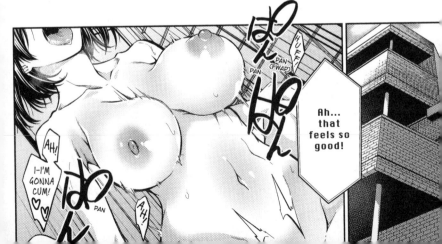

PAN (FWAP)

HUFF!

PAN

PAN

AH!

I-I'M GONNA CUM!

AH!

Ah... that feels so good!

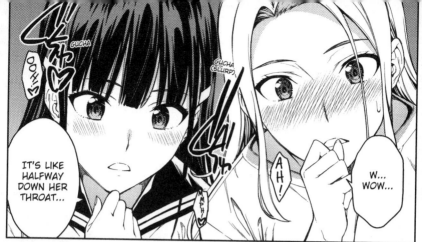

GUCHA

OOH! ♡

GUCHA
SLURP!

AH!

MMPH! ♡

IT'S LIKE HALFWAY DOWN HER THROAT...

W... WOW...

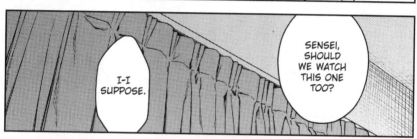

I-I SUPPOSE.

SENSEI, SHOULD WE WATCH THIS ONE TOO?

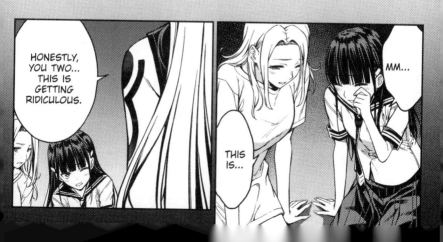

HONESTLY, YOU TWO... THIS IS GETTING RIDICULOUS.

THIS IS...

MM...

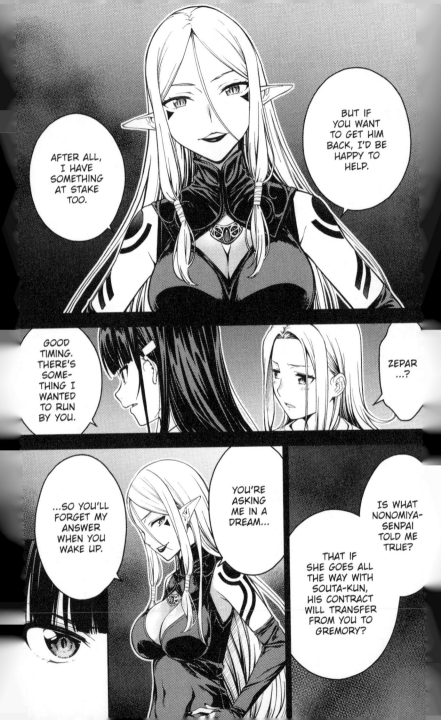

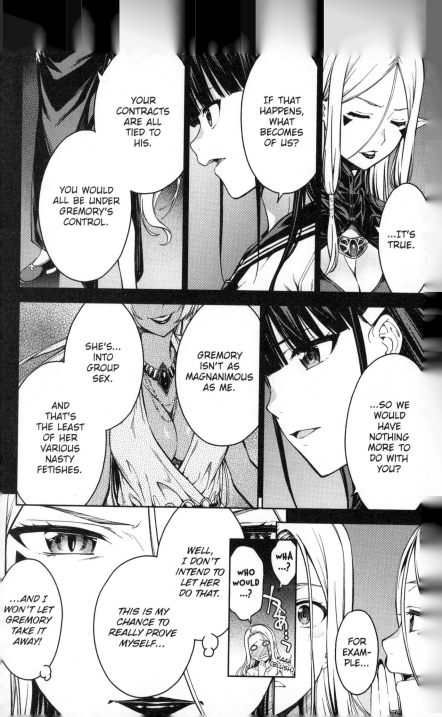

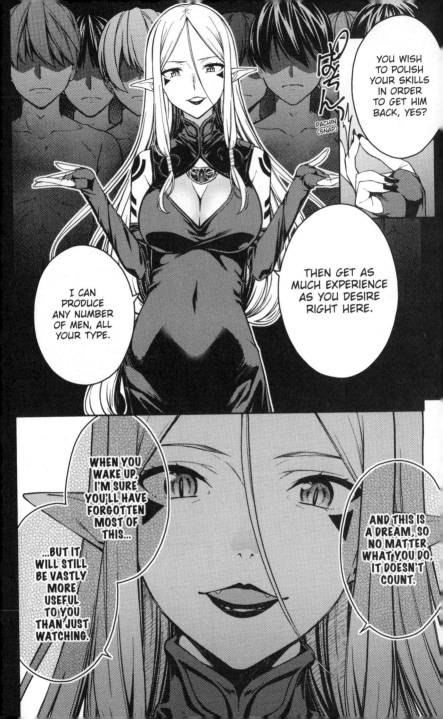

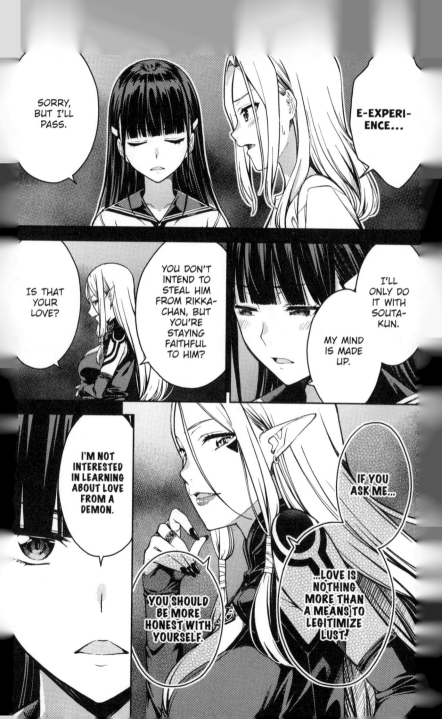

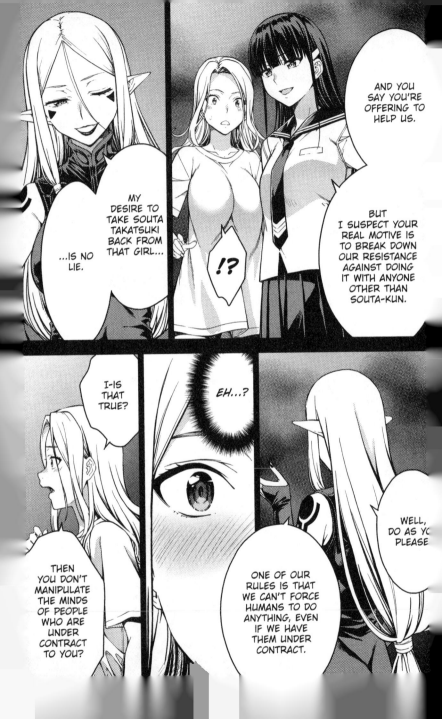

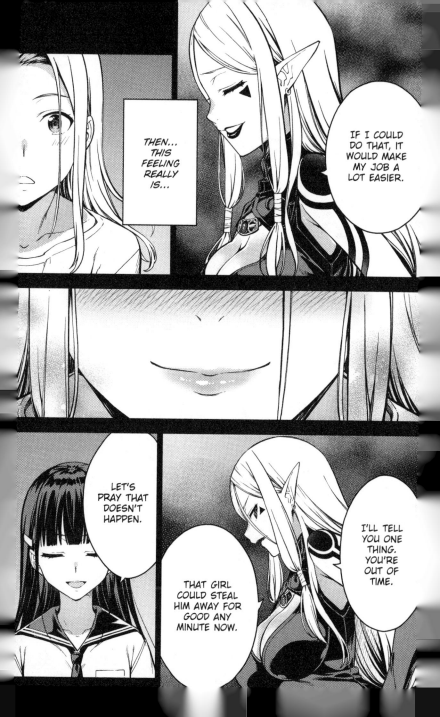

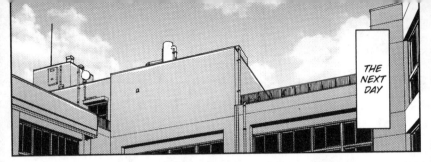

THE NEXT DAY

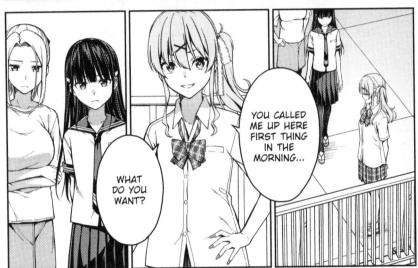

YOU CALLED ME UP HERE FIRST THING IN THE MORNING...

WHAT DO YOU WANT?

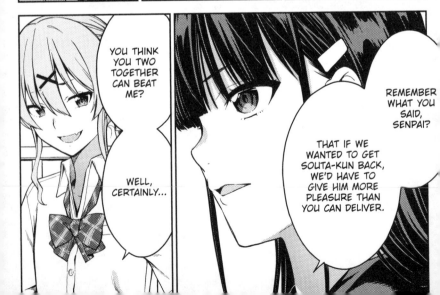

YOU THINK YOU TWO TOGETHER CAN BEAT ME?

WELL, CERTAINLY...

REMEMBER WHAT YOU SAID, SENPAI?

THAT IF WE WANTED TO GET SOUTA-KUN BACK, WE'D HAVE TO GIVE HIM MORE PLEASURE THAN YOU CAN DELIVER.

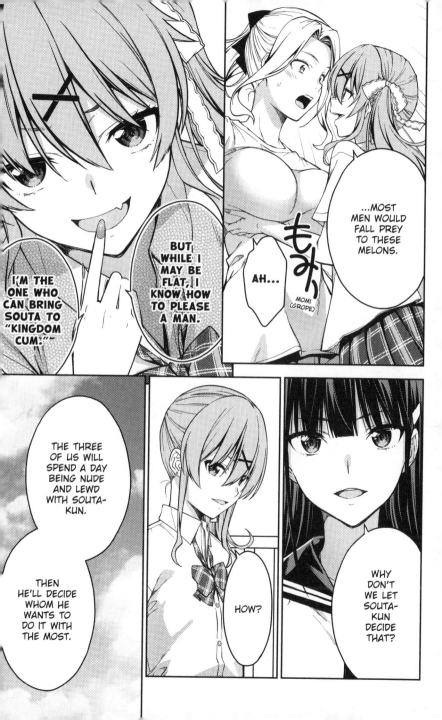

I'M THE ONE WHO CAN BRING SOUTA TO "KINGDOM CUM."

BUT WHILE I MAY BE FLAT, I KNOW HOW TO PLEASE A MAN.

...MOST MEN WOULD FALL PREY TO THESE MELONS.

AH...

もみ, (GROPE)

THE THREE OF US WILL SPEND A DAY BEING NUDE AND LEWD WITH SOUTA-KUN.

THEN HE'LL DECIDE WHOM HE WANTS TO DO IT WITH THE MOST.

HOW?

WHY DON'T WE LET SOUTA-KUN DECIDE THAT?

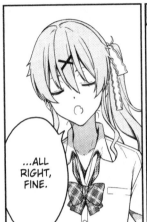

...ALL RIGHT, FINE.

I DON'T THINK SOUTA-KUN WOULD REFUSE THAT OFFER.

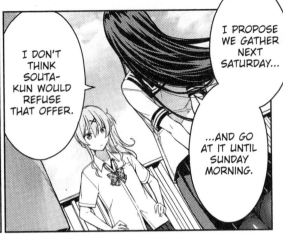

I PROPOSE WE GATHER NEXT SATURDAY...

...AND GO AT IT UNTIL SUNDAY MORNING.

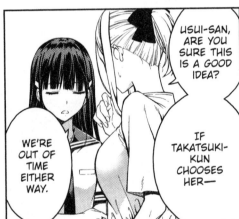

USUI-SAN, ARE YOU SURE THIS IS A GOOD IDEA?

IF TAKATSUKI-KUN CHOOSES HER—

WE'RE OUT OF TIME EITHER WAY.

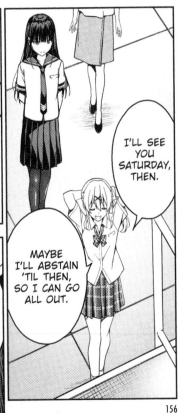

I'LL SEE YOU SATURDAY, THEN.

MAYBE I'LL ABSTAIN 'TIL THEN, SO I CAN GO ALL OUT.

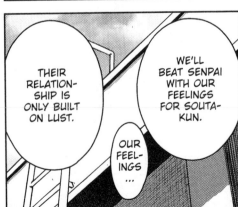

THEIR RELATION-SHIP IS ONLY BUILT ON LUST.

WE'LL BEAT SENPAI WITH OUR FEELINGS FOR SOUTA-KUN.

OUR FEEL-INGS...

156

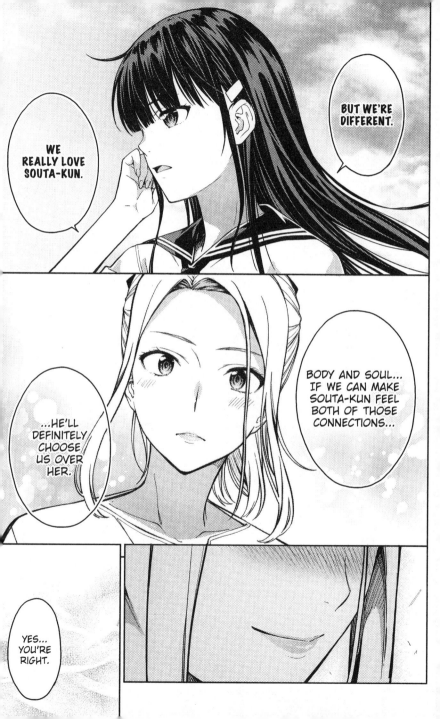

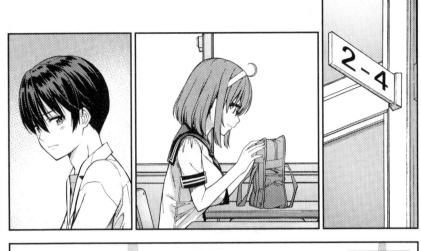

2-4

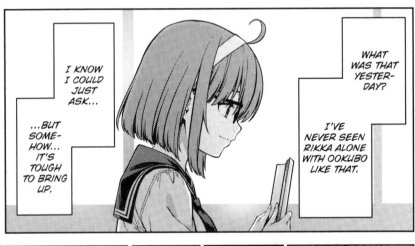

WHAT WAS THAT YESTER-DAY?

I'VE NEVER SEEN RIKKA ALONE WITH OOKUBO LIKE THAT.

I KNOW I COULD JUST ASK...

...BUT SOME-HOW... IT'S TOUGH TO BRING UP.

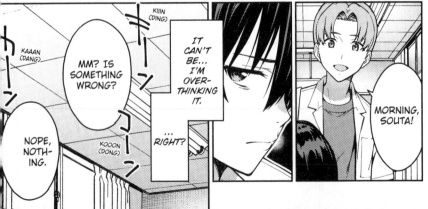

KIIIN
(DING)

KAAAN
(DANG)

MM? IS SOMETHING WRONG?

IT CAN'T BE... I'M OVER-THINKING IT.

...RIGHT?

MORNING, SOUTA!

NOPE, NOTH-ING.

KOOON
(DONG)

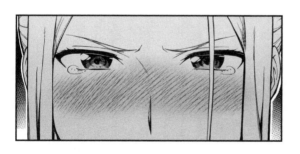

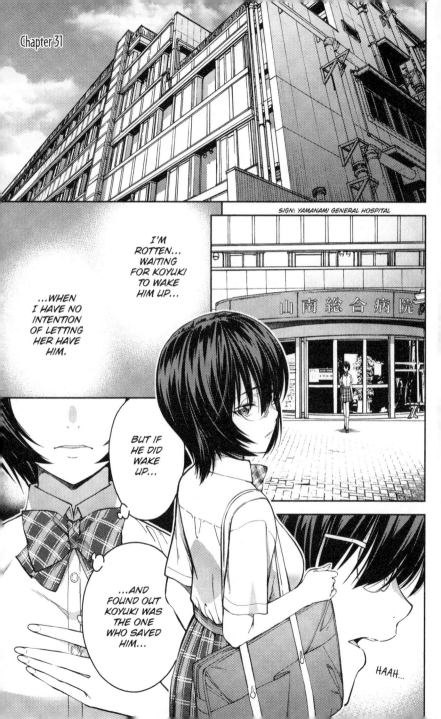

SIGN: YAMANAMI GENERAL HOSPITAL

I'M ROTTEN... WAITING FOR KOYUKI TO WAKE HIM UP...

...WHEN I HAVE NO INTENTION OF LETTING HER HAVE HIM.

BUT IF HE DID WAKE UP...

...AND FOUND OUT KOYUKI WAS THE ONE WHO SAVED HIM...

HAAH...

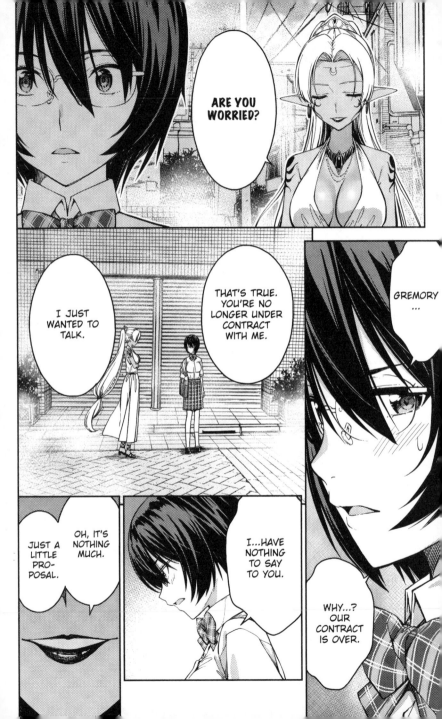

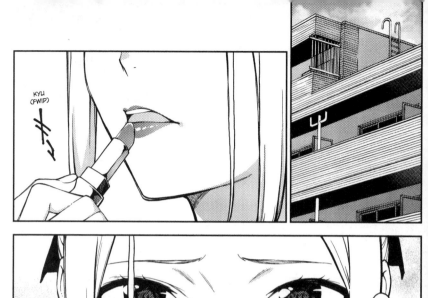

KYU
(FWIP)

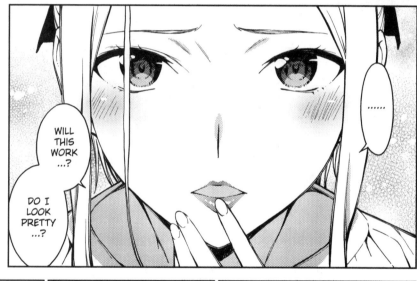

WILL THIS WORK ...?

DO I LOOK PRETTY ...?

......

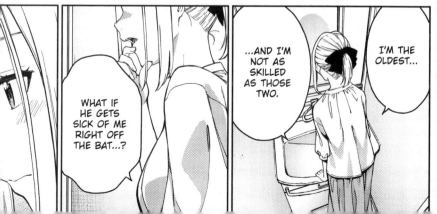

WHAT IF HE GETS SICK OF ME RIGHT OFF THE BAT...?

...AND I'M NOT AS SKILLED AS THOSE TWO.

I'M THE OLDEST...

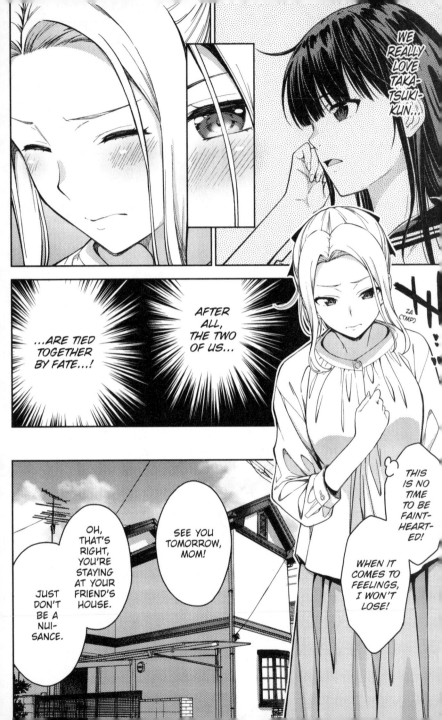

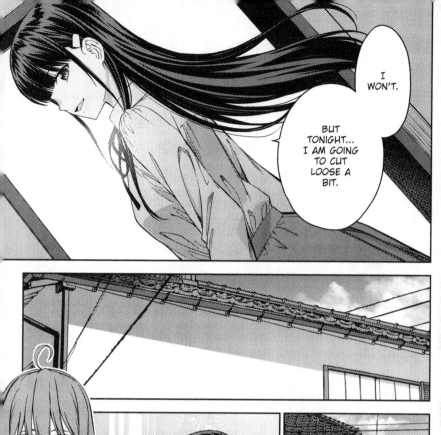

I WON'T.

BUT TONIGHT... I AM GOING TO CUT LOOSE A BIT.

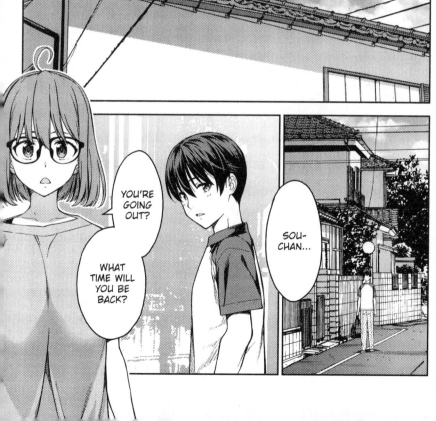

YOU'RE GOING OUT?

WHAT TIME WILL YOU BE BACK?

SOU-CHAN...

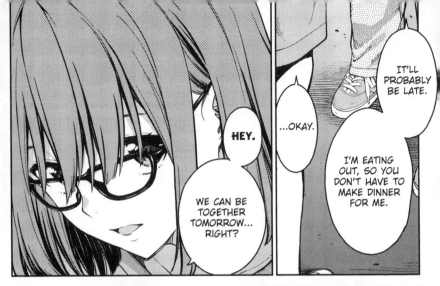

IT'LL PROBABLY BE LATE.

...OKAY.

HEY.

I'M EATING OUT, SO YOU DON'T HAVE TO MAKE DINNER FOR ME.

WE CAN BE TOGETHER TOMORROW... RIGHT?

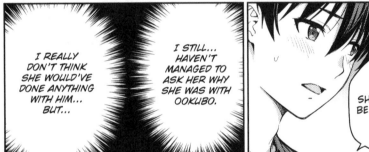

I REALLY DON'T THINK SHE WOULD'VE DONE ANYTHING WITH HIM... BUT...

I STILL... HAVEN'T MANAGED TO ASK HER WHY SHE WAS WITH OOKUBO.

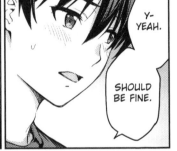

Y-YEAH.

SHOULD BE FINE.

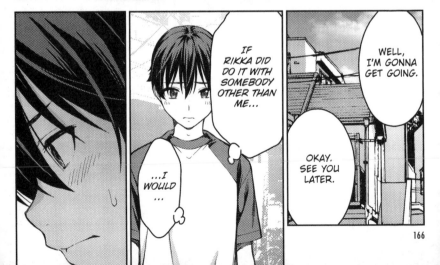

IF RIKKA DID DO IT WITH SOMEBODY OTHER THAN ME...

....I WOULD...

WELL, I'M GONNA GET GOING.

OKAY. SEE YOU LATER.

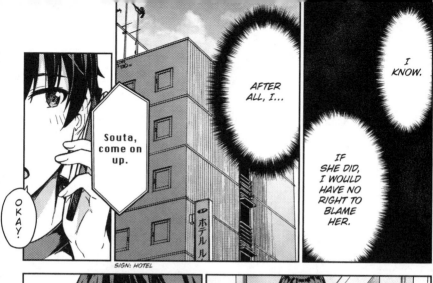

I KNOW.

AFTER ALL, I...

IF SHE DID, I WOULD HAVE NO RIGHT TO BLAME HER.

Souta, come on up.

OKAY!

SIGN: HOTEL

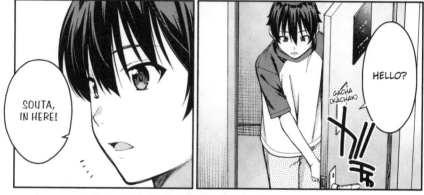

SOUTA, IN HERE!

GACHA (KACHAK)

HELLO?

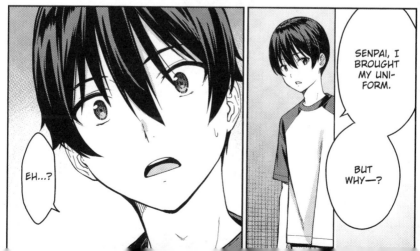

SENPAI, I BROUGHT MY UNI-FORM.

BUT WHY—?

EH...?

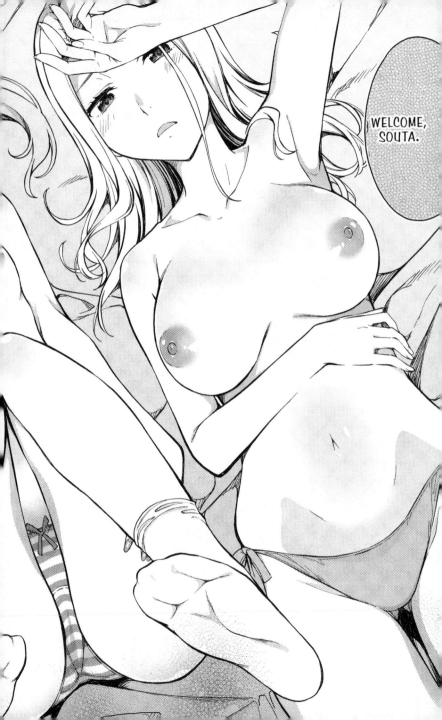

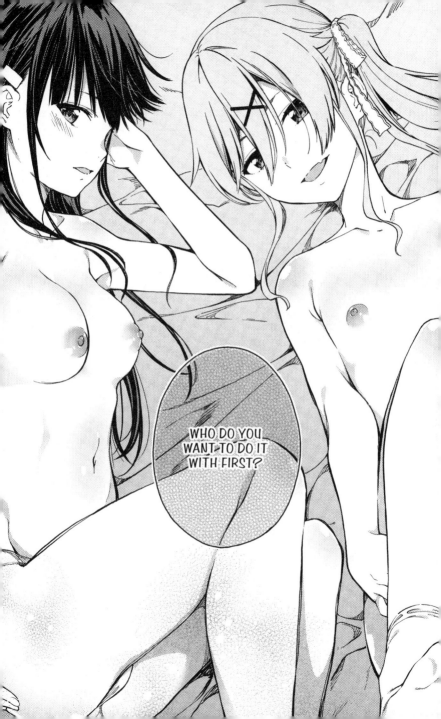

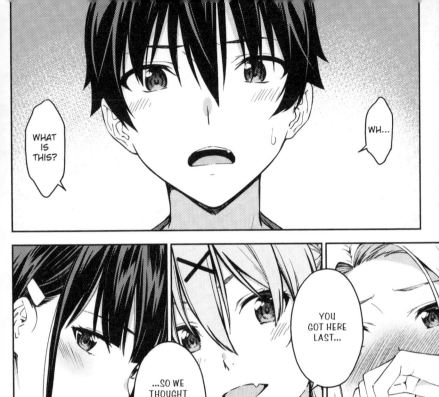

WHAT IS THIS?

WH...

YOU GOT HERE LAST...

...SO WE THOUGHT WE WOULD SURPRISE YOU.

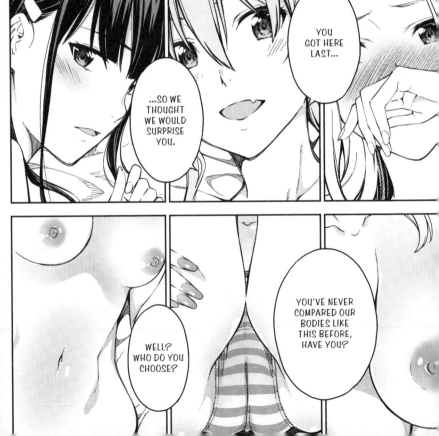

WELL? WHO DO YOU CHOOSE?

YOU'VE NEVER COMPARED OUR BODIES LIKE THIS BEFORE, HAVE YOU?

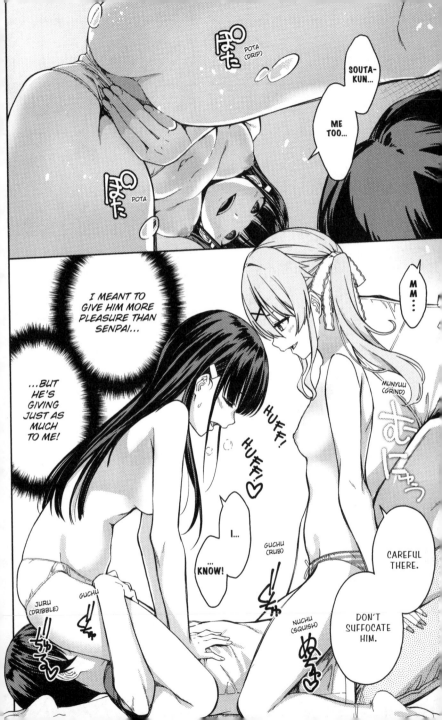

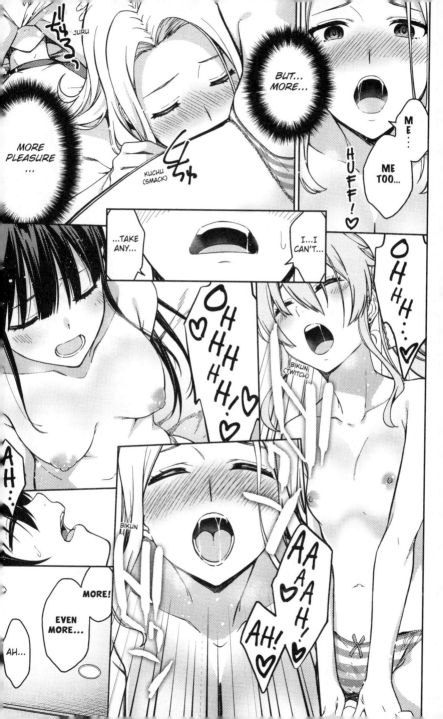

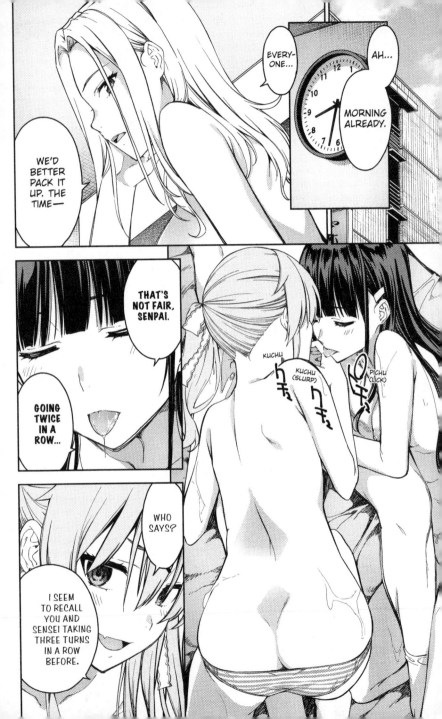

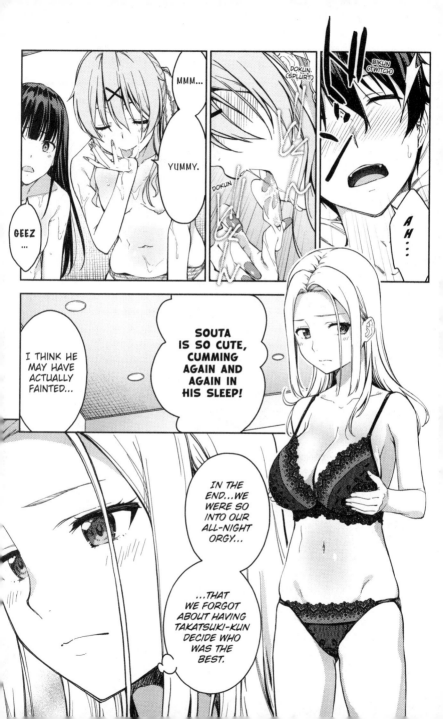

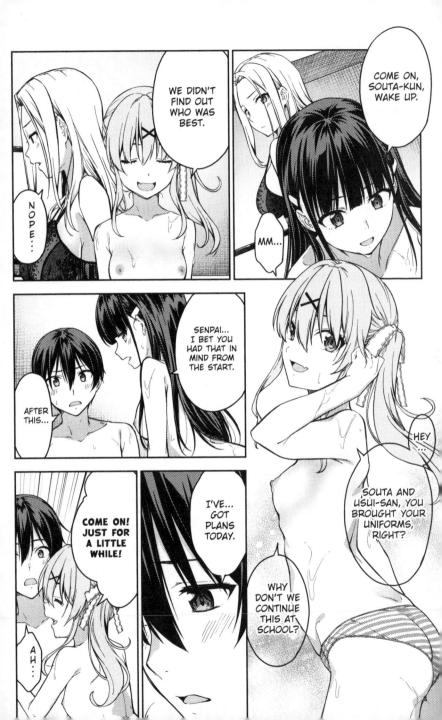

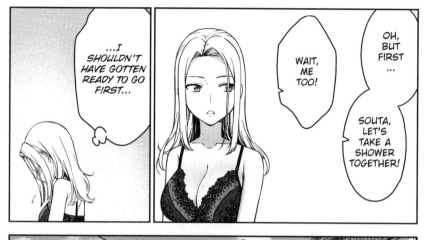

...I SHOULDN'T HAVE GOTTEN READY TO GO FIRST...

WAIT, ME TOO!

OH, BUT FIRST...

SOUTA, LET'S TAKE A SHOWER TOGETHER!

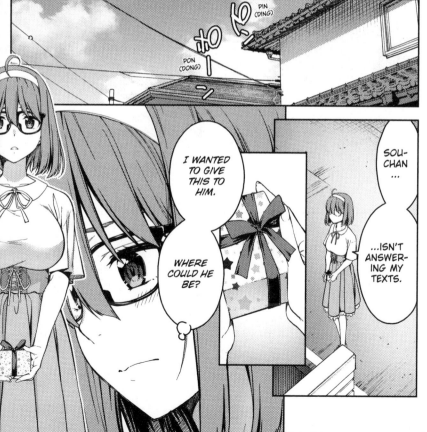

PIN (DING)

PON (DONG)

I WANTED TO GIVE THIS TO HIM.

WHERE COULD HE BE?

SOU-CHAN...

...ISN'T ANSWERING MY TEXTS.

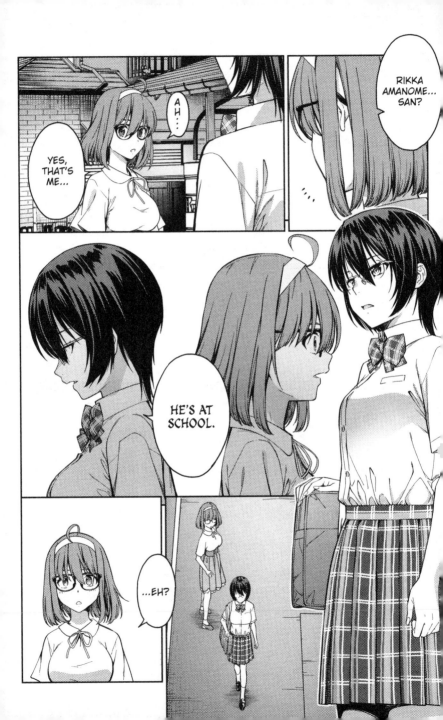

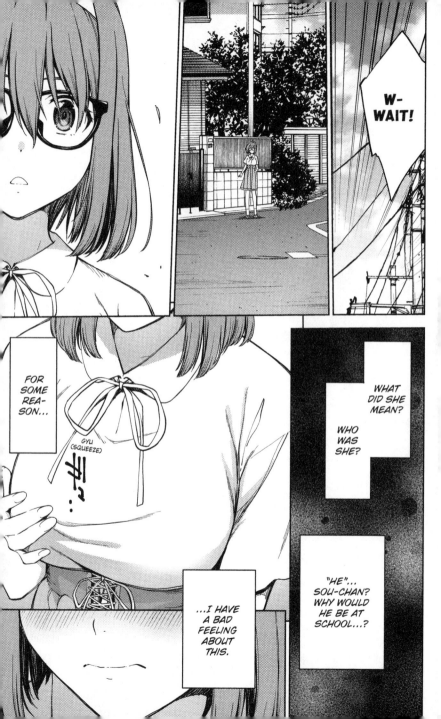

W-WAIT!

FOR SOME REA-SON...

GYU (SQUEEZE)

...I HAVE A BAD FEELING ABOUT THIS.

WHAT DID SHE MEAN?

WHO WAS SHE?

"HE"... SOU-CHAN? WHY WOULD HE BE AT SCHOOL...?

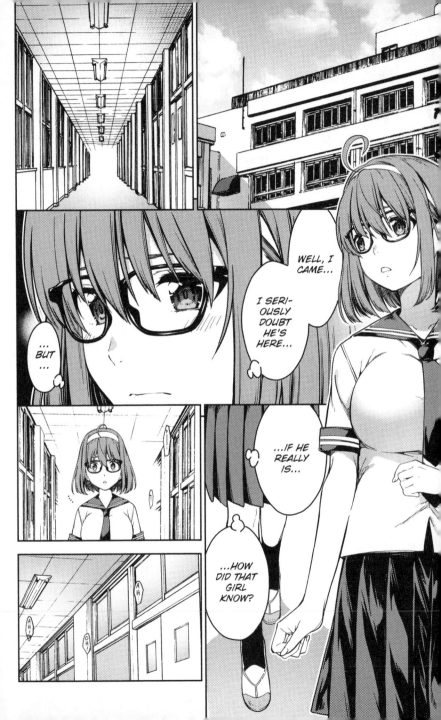

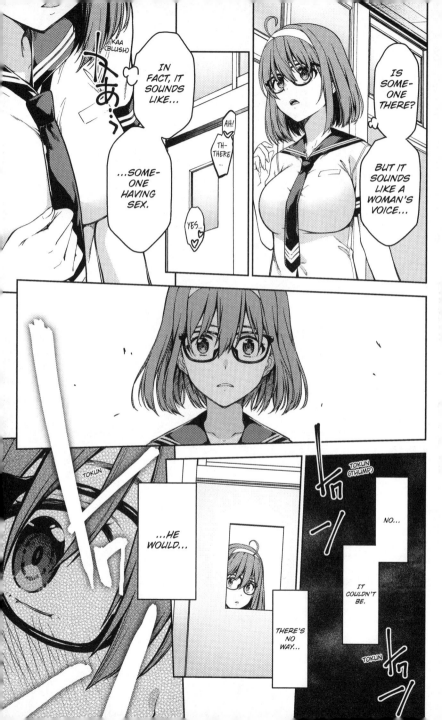

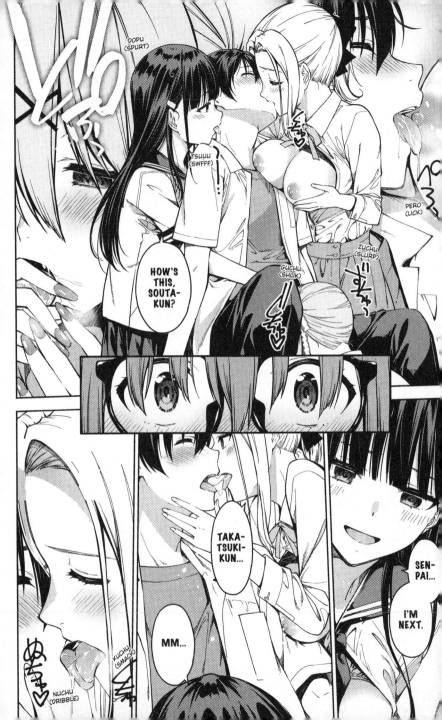

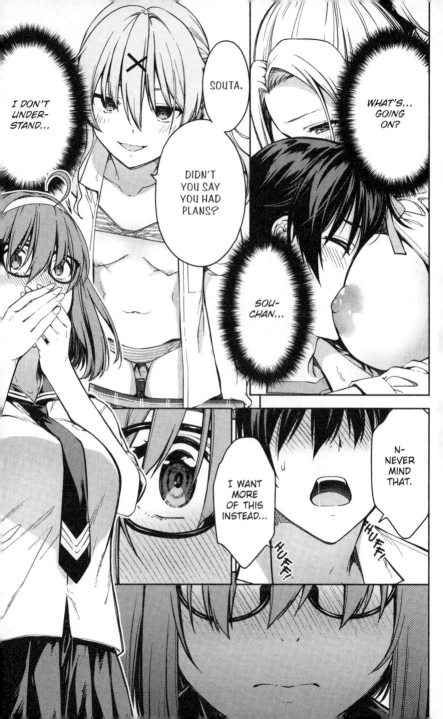

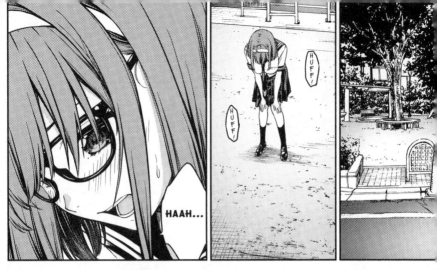

HAAH...

HUFF!

HUFF!

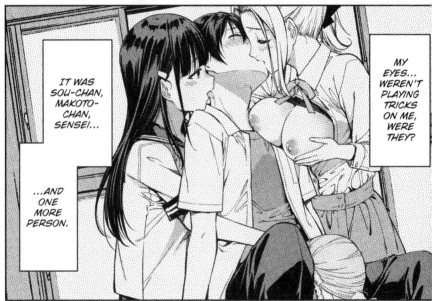

IT WAS SOU-CHAN, MAKOTO-CHAN, SENSEI...

...AND ONE MORE PERSON.

MY EYES... WEREN'T PLAYING TRICKS ON ME, WERE THEY?

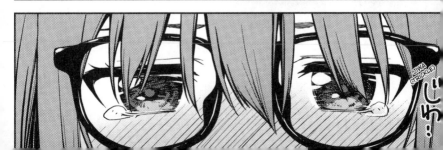

JIWA (TRICKLE)

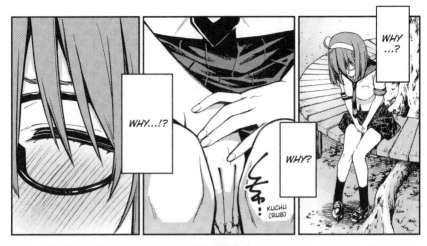

WHY...!?

WHY?

KUCHU
(RUB)

WHY
...?

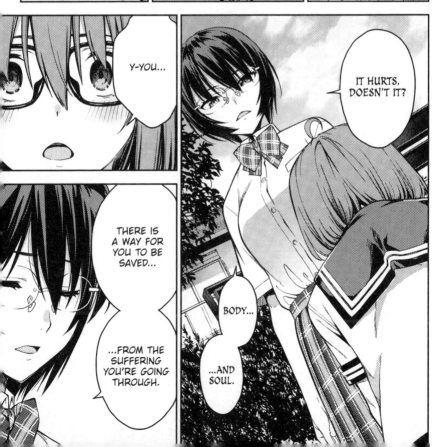

Y-YOU...

IT HURTS,
DOESN'T IT?

THERE IS
A WAY FOR
YOU TO BE
SAVED...

...FROM THE
SUFFERING
YOU'RE GOING
THROUGH.

BODY...

...AND
SOUL.

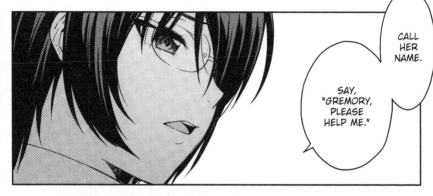

CALL HER NAME.

SAY, "GREMORY, PLEASE HELP ME."

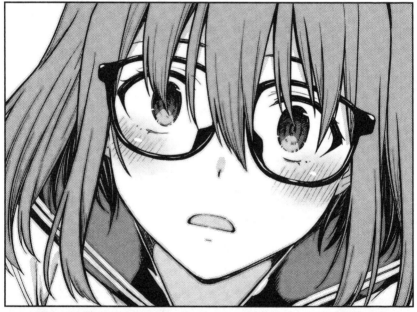

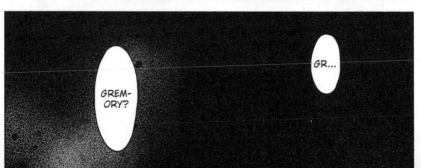

GR...

GREMORY?

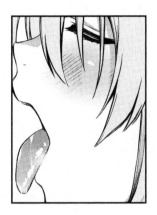

● Staff ●

The author
Osamu Takahashi

Assistant
Miki

Japanese edition design
Emi Nakano (BANANA GROVE STUDIO)

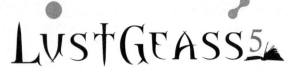

LUST GEASS 5

Osamu Takahashi

TRANSLATION: Sheldon Drzka • LETTERING: Phil Christie

LUST GEASS, Vol. 5
©Osamu Takahashi 2021
First published in Japan in 2021 by KADOKAWA CORPORATION, Tokyo.
English translation rights arranged with KADOKAWA CORPORATION, Tokyo through TUTTLE-MORI AGENCY, INC., Tokyo.

English translation © 2022 by Yen Press, LLC

Yen Press
150 West 30th Street, 19th Floor
New York, NY 10001

Visit us at yenpress.com • facebook.com/yenpress • twitter.com/yenpress • yenpress.tumblr.com • instagram.com/yenpress

First Yen Press Edition: March 2022

Yen Press is an imprint of Yen Press, LLC.
The Yen Press name and logo are trademarks of Yen Press, LLC.

Library of Congress Control Number: 2020933605

ISBNs: 978-1-9753-3870-1 (paperback)
       978-1-9753-3871-8 (ebook)

10 9 8 7 6 5 4 3 2 1

LSC-C

Printed in the United States of America

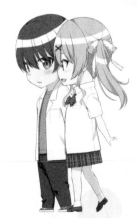